Into The Crucible

Into The Crucible
Making Marines for the 21st Century

James B. Woulfe

PRESIDIO

Even though I am a commissioned officer in the U.S. Marine Corps, the writing of this book was done entirely on my own time. The contents of this book should not be construed as representing the official policies or positions of the U.S. Department of Defense, the U.S. Department of the Navy, or the U.S. Marine Corps. The opinions expressed herein are my own, as are any errors or omissions.

Copyright © 1998 James B. Woulfe

Published by Presidio Press
505 B San Marin Drive, Suite 300
Novato, CA 94945-1340

Library of Congress Cataloging-in-Publication Data

Woulfe, James B., 1968–
Into the crucible : making Marines for the 21st century / James B. Woulfe.
p.   cm.
Includes bibliographical references and index.
ISBN: 0-89141-707-9 (softcover)
ISBN: 0-89141-657-9 (hardcover)
1. Basic training (Military education)—United States. 2. United States.
Marine Corps—History—20th century. I. Title.
VE432.W68   1998
359.9'65'0973—dc21   98-2708
                                            CIP

All photos courtesy U.S. Marine Corps

Printed in the United States of America

To the Marines who gave their lives serving our great nation.

Contents

Acknowledgments

I could probably go on forever thanking people who made this book possible, but I'll try to make it short. First, my mother and my wife have both been huge influences in my life. My mother was a single parent raising two rambunctious boys, and she did an amazing job under the most demanding circumstances. I have no idea how she did it, but I'm so grateful for her model of strength I can't begin to describe it. My wife is the most wonderful friend I could ever imagine. Those who are fortunate enough to know her, know that she is truly my "better half." It's not only her support, but her example that I really benefit from.

A special thank you to the staff at Presidio Press, especially Bob Kane and E. J. McCarthy.

Finally, I must thank my fellow Marines. Their hard work and dedication motivated me to improve my writing skills and I never would have been able to write this book if it were not for them. Naming all of them and the reasons for my thanks would be a book in itself, so I'll just mention three important groups: my recruiters who gave me the straight scoop; my drill instructors who tirelessly labored to transform me into a Marine during the summer of 1986; and, the exceptional Marines of Drill Instructor School, MCRD, San Diego, with whom I served while I wrote this book. It's Marines like these who make the Corps great. Each provided far more for me than I ever could for them, and I am eternally grateful.

Foreword

In a large organization, one whose roots are deep in the substance of the nation, change is necessarily slow—almost glacial. The stakes involved in the evolution of an institution like the United States Marine Corps, where people are the prime coin, make it essential that any major change be studied, tested, and proven before exposing it to the bulk of the Corps.

And that characterizes the growth of the Crucible, a major fifty-four-hour challenge designed to underscore the preceding eleven demanding weeks of recruit training, to test, to the ultimate, the recruits' minds and their bodies, to emphasize the qualities of reliability, loyalty, honesty, resolution, patriotism and teamwork to which they have been subjected in the weeks just past. Limitations on food and rest, physical demands and decision-making requirements invariably involving teamwork, all characterize the Crucible as the classic culminating event of a rigorous revolution in the recruit's life. If they cannot survive the Crucible, their career in the Marine Corps is in doubt.

To add substance to the Crucible it was seen as necessary that everyone involved in the undertaking understand it perfectly. Thus, drill instructors are subjected to the same challenges as the recruit for whom they are responsible, as are officers who have direct responsibility for the Crucible's conduct, as well as noncommissioned officers in the units to which the recruit is to be assigned on graduation.

To make the demands of the Crucible more meaningful to those subjected to it, each major requirement is framed on the performance of a well-known Marine Corps hero—Medal of Honor winners of years past. Jim Woulfe has woven these inspiring historical recitals into a matrix that tells a story that has to impress every reader, Marine and civilian alike. In that sense, the book turns out to be more than a description of an important development in Marine training, but encapsulates, as well, both the history and the ethos of a great American institution. *Semper Fidelis!*

Victor H. Krulak
Lieutenant General, USMC (Ret.)

Preface

After toying with the idea of this book for several months, I finally sat down to begin writing on a Memorial Day weekend. It seemed an appropriate way to recognize our dead servicemen and women. Unfortunately, there was also a personal twist that made it even more poignant. A family friend with whom I shared childhood memories, the wife of a Marine helicopter pilot, was widowed just a few days before. The Marine died in the prime of life when his Cobra helicopter lost power and fell to earth. It was a most tragic story, probably told before and would be again: a wife without her partner, a daughter who would never again feel the loving embrace of her father, and an unborn boy that would never have the opportunity.

I never met him, but I recognize him as a brother; those who have never served may not understand how this is possible. Our only interactions were over the telephone, but the conversations always were natural and too long considering we'd never met face to face, a testimony to the commonality Marines find in one another. He was a few years behind me in terms of career, so I could provide insight of what lay ahead while he reminded me of where I'd been.

A major television network started its nightly news during this same Memorial Day with a story about the latest film to hit movie screens. *It was their lead story!* The Memorial Day recognition was placed somewhere toward the end of the newscast, almost as an afterthought. There seemed to be no significance to the day other than another opportunity to sleep late, miss work, or go to the movies. Was our nation grateful for the sacrifices service members made on the battlefield and in training areas? Did Americans care? I was personally disgusted by the time the news ended, questioning whether there was anything really worth fighting and risking death for.

My self-pity means little and I can quickly snap out of it when I review the enormous acts of courage demonstrated by the Medal of Honor recipients and other heroes mentioned in the pages of this book. The Marine Corps motto *(Semper Fidelis)* empowers me to believe that as long as there are Marines, the same courage will continue. Their actions will never be duplicated exactly, but I am confident the heroic spirit embodied in each of them will be played out on the battlefields of the future. It's what Marines do.

If I could ask for one thing from my fellow Americans, it would be that they never forget that there is a group of men and women, average on any scale of ability, but poised to take on challenges that stretch human capability to its limits. After spending my entire adult life as a Marine, and three years watching drill instructors make Marines at the Recruit Depot in San Diego, I am convinced that there is nothing special about those who enlist in our Corps. You could switch a bus full of recruits headed to Marine boot camp with that of another service and the results would still be the same at graduation. Marine Corps recruits are average Americans from the streets and the high schools of our country, but they are Americans who dared to dream that they could be something. That dream combines with the reality of a Marine Corps drill instructor to create a transformation from which we all benefit, because Marines who complete recruit training are far better Americans than when they began. The beautiful part about this process is that the drill instructor was also a recruit just a few years ago. A continuum that is never ending: the passing of tradition and a commitment to excellence from the old Corps to the new.

These "average" few are Marines who will carry the burden of our future forward, on their own backs if necessary. While we may commemorate the greatness of the events highlighted in the media, and the individuals who achieve them, we can never forget the sacrifice of those who made it all possible. We live in a country where I am safe to write a book like this freely, without fear of censor or retaliation from some government agency. Regardless of our personal opinions, the fact is that we Americans may disagree among ourselves on any street corner or in any periodical. These freedoms may seem commonplace to us, but are beyond comprehension for citizens of some other countries.

From my own experiences in the jungles of the Philippines, streets of Los Angeles ('92 riots), frozen hills of Korea, deserts of Kuwait, and the wasteland of Somalia, Marines continue to rekindle my faith in this country. While I read newspaper accounts and watch television programs that depress me about the state of our youth, I go to work and see our fabulous enlisted Marines that really represent America. Someone out there is doing something right.

I would be remiss if I did not point out that the Marines graduating from recruit training are not "average." By the time they graduate from recruit training they are very different. The reasons for their being special are not tangible traits that can be summarized on paper with statistics, but those who have spent time around Marines know what I mean. I am completely in awe of their performance in even the most stressful and demanding situations. I consider myself privileged to have had the opportunity to serve with such men and women. *Semper Fidelis!*

Those intimately familiar with Marine Corps recruit training will probably notice slight differences between their experience and my description of the Crucible. This could be the result of many things, but most likely it is due to the event being in an eternal state of evolution. The Crucible can never be finalized, because what was successful yesterday may not work today nor prepare us for tomorrow. Minor details and specific methods must change to maximize the effectiveness of the course. One obvious example is a change that occurred just prior to the book's publication; recruits stopped calling their drill instructors by rank during the Crucible and continued to call them "sir" or "ma'am." Addressing Marines by rank is now reserved for the end of the event, after the recruit earns the title of Marine. Though this may seem insignificant, it strengthens the transformation from civilian to Marine by giving the drill instructor another way to reinforce to the new Marine that he or she is truly different. And this highlights the fact that the Crucible does not actually make Marines—drill instructors do.

Introduction

In late 1775 the Second Continental Congress sat in Philadelphia and debated the need to establish a Continental Navy. Full-scale war with the British was a reality, and the Continental Army could not be victorious without support from the sea. The question of Marines was raised: *If there was going to be a Navy, would not there then be the need for Marines?* Half seaman and half soldier, Marines were basically infantrymen detailed to sea duty, but not expected to sail the ship. They assisted the captain in maintaining order and discipline aboard the vessel, but also turned their bayonets toward the enemy as boarding parties and landing forces when the need arose.

The answer was obvious: *Yes, there must be Marines!* A committee was raised, a resolution offered, and on 10 November 1775, it was passed by the Congress:

> Resolved, that two Battalions of Marines be raised consisting of one Colonel, two Lieutenant Colonels, two Majors and Officers as usual in other regiments, that they consist of an equal number of privates with other battalions; that particular care be taken that no person be appointed to office or enlisted into said Battalions, but such as are good seamen, or so acquainted with maritime affairs as to be able to serve advantage by sea, when required. That they be enlisted and commissioned for and during the present war between Great Britain and the colonies, unless dismissed by order of Congress. That they be distinguished by the name of the first and second battalions of American Marines, and that they consider

1

a part of the number, which the Continental Army before
Boston is ordered to consist of.

The president of the congress, John Hancock, signed a captain's
commission on 28 November, making Samuel Nicholas the first Marine officer. The challenge that lay before him continues today: to
recruit qualified individuals to serve as Marines. Nicholas's family
owned a tavern, not the background expected for the leader of a
maritime fighting force, but an important qualification for the new
recruiting effort. An early poster said: TAKE COURAGE THEN, SEIZE THE
FORTUNE THAT AWAITS YOU, REPAIR TO THE MARINE RENDEZVOUS, WHERE
IN A FLOWING BOWL OF [rum] PUNCH, AND THREE TIMES THREE, YOU
SHALL DRINK.

By late December 1775, five detachments were raised consisting
of a collection of semiskilled and unskilled laborers in their teens
and midtwenties. One roster provides insight into the quality of the
new recruits, with only eight of the forty-one being native-born
Americans. Also, in complete disregard for the direction set forth in
the Congressional resolution, none claimed any knowledge of life
at sea or naval warfare. With these new recruits came another challenge that continues today—to make Marines.

In the beginning there was no formal Marine Corps recruit training. New members learned their trade through the use of "rookie
squads" and on-the-job training supervised by seasoned privates at various posts and stations. There were attempts to formalize the training as early as 1805, when Lt. Col. Franklin Wharton (commandant
1804–1818) tried to standardize how Marines were trained to shoot
and march. He organized a school for recruits at the Marine Barracks
in Washington, D.C., covering up to two months of rudimentary training in drill, manual of arms, and marksmanship. Those first recruits
who fell in on the "yellow footprints" were often illiterate, unfamil-
iar with the English language, younger than the recruits of today, and
trained by men not much different from themselves. The commandant's idea was revolutionary, but also impossible to implement with
the limited funds and qualified trainers available. It soon faded away.

Several of Lieutenant Colonel Wharton's successors attempted to
revive recruit training, but none had much luck during the 1800s.

Colonel Archibald Henderson (commandant 1820–1859), the "grand old man of the Corps" (so nicknamed because of his more than fifty years of service), was the most successful at enhancing the entry-level training his Marines received. Unfortunately, the same old reason of not enough money prevented extensive improvements. Another obstacle was the lack of a national transportation system to transport recruits to centralized locations. The completion of the transcontinental railroad on 10 May 1869, changed that. When the tracks of the Union Pacific joined those of the Central Pacific at Promontory Point, Utah, the Corps could begin the process of standardizing recruit training.

It was not until a full century after Commandant Wharton, in 1911, that formal Marine Corps Recruit Training was established. The Marines' fame during operations in China, Nicaragua, Mexico, and the Philippines at the beginning of the century led to increases in the numbers joining. That, along with the need to provide better training on the new M1903 Springfield rifle, made recruit training a practical necessity. The country now had the infrastructure needed to transport recruits effectively to training locations. The transformation of young Americans into the world's premier fighting men became official.

At first, an eight-week schedule of drill, physical training, close combat, and marksmanship began at recruit depots in Philadelphia, Norfolk, Puget Sound, and Mare Island (California). These locations made sense, being at the seacoasts of the country and within reach of major ports. Eventually, recruit training would be centralized at depots at Parris Island, South Carolina (established in 1915), and Mare Island.

During World War I, the training was specifically designed to prepare a recruit for the trenches of France in an eight-to-ten-week course. The strength of the Corps was about 10,000 in 1916, but it would be over 75,000 by 1918. The depots at Parris Island and Mare Island were soon bursting at the seams, making it necessary to establish temporary training sites at the Philadelphia, Brooklyn, and Norfolk Navy Yards. It was the first real test of recruit training, one that the Corps passed with flying colors. The performance of Marines in action against the Germans became legendary, thrusting the

Corps into the light of international attention. Before the war, the Corps was mostly limited to service with small detachments on ships and naval installations, but now they were "Devil Dogs," the name the Germans gave to the Marines during the battle of Belleau Wood to describe their tenacity in combat—*Teufelhunden!*

In 1923, the Marine Corps Recruit Depot at San Diego was established. Today, San Diego and Parris Island remain the two boot camps where Marine recruits are trained. Although both produce warriors, the two are like fraternal twins who are complete opposites. Parris Island seems isolated, located across the tidal swamps of Archer Creek. The uniform of the day is usually camouflage utilities because of the severe weather conditions. San Diego on the other hand, is surrounded by development, seems always to have a number of visitors on board, and sits adjacent to the city's airport. Camouflage utilities are rarely worn in San Diego, with one version or another of the dress or service uniform being preferred. Graduates of each like to claim that one is better than the other, but there has never been any truth to the assertions. Both are equally effective at producing Marines. Regardless of their differences, it's impossible to identify where a Marine was trained without asking.

Between the World Wars, the Great Depression forced the use of indoctrination training to make up for the sparse resources. The force hovered around 17,000 for this period, but Marines were still to be found in harm's way. As Maj. Gen. Smedley Butler put it, "Marines are given orders, and they go."[1] They were ashore many times throughout the Caribbean, some fighting bandits during the "Banana Wars" in Haiti and the Dominican Republic. Others protected the stability of the Canal Zone with landings in Panama, Cuba, and Mexico, as well as preserving democracy with occupation duties in Nicaragua. The jungle experiences would prove to be valuable in the near future, as would basic techniques developed for close air support and amphibious operations.

1. Moskin, J. Robert, *The U.S. Marine Corps Story*, 3d Edition, (New York, McGraw Hill, 1992) 149. Quoting Lowell Thomas, *Old Gimlet Eye: The Adventures of Smedley D. Butler* (New York, Farrar & Rinehart, 1933) 170.

In the late 1930s there were only 300 recruits a month at Parris Island, making it look more like a ghost town than a military base, but after the attack on Pearl Harbor, the depots exploded as the Corps began its climb from about 54,000 Marines in 1941 to over 485,000 in 1945. More than 450,000 passed through the gates of the depots at Parris Island and San Diego. With the large numbers also came the need to be more productive, and recruit training became more efficient and organized. The endless stream of recruits marched across the parade deck to become Marines, quickly deploying to the Pacific to fight the Japanese. From the results on the battlefield, it is safe to assume that recruit training was successful. The Corps was recognized, again, as one of the world's premier fighting forces. Admiral Chester Nimitz said it best, "Uncommon valor was a common virtue," in describing the Marines' fight for Iwo Jima.

The post–World War II military cuts resulted in the Corps' strength dropping to around 75,000 officers and enlisted, causing manpower turmoil when the Korean conflict began. Privates first class had to be assigned as senior drill instructors, but the Corps continued to live up to the legend.

Outnumbered South Korean, American, and other United Nations forces were forced to defend a small portion of the peninsula called the Pusan Perimeter, causing Army general Douglas MacArthur to exclaim: "If only I had the 1st Marine Division," a wish he was granted. The Marines' amphibious assault at Inchon put the allies back on the offensive and sent the North Koreans fleeing back across the thirty-eighth parallel.

By the end of the war, recruit training was ten weeks and a formal school for drill instructors was a permanent part of the depots' organization.

Shortly after the Korean War, tragedy hit the Corps when six recruits drowned at Parris Island. Their drill instructor, SSgt. Matthew McKeon, was upset at their platoon's poor performance the day before and decided to march them through the swollen waters of Ribbon Creek on the night of 8 April 1956. They walked into a fish hole, causing panic among the recruits. That incident caused immediate changes in the way recruit training was supervised, with additional commissioned officers being assigned to the depots.

The 1960s produced a war in Vietnam, which would become more and more unpopular as the decade wore on. Another huge increase in the number of Marines needed from the depots became evident, but the Corps was better prepared after the experiences of World War I, World War II, and Korea. Unfortunately, lower enlistment standards from programs like "McNamara's Hundred Thousand" made the drill instructors' job even harder. Incidents of abuse increased during recruit training, corrected by the Corps as observed, but the country's attention was focused on the battles overseas. Marines fought the Vietcong and the North Vietnamese from the streets of Hue to the hilly jungle outside Khe Sanh. As usual, the Devil Dogs performed with gallantry and distinction, adding new chapters to the Marine legend.

The "all-volunteer" force of the seventies was a mixed blessing. The people's resentment toward Vietnam, coupled with a poor public image of the military, caused recruiters to enlist some who brought with them many problems. "Join the Corps or go to jail" was uttered by judges across the country, which again made life difficult for drill instructors. Then another disaster struck with two deaths and several abuse allegations in late 1975 and early 1976. The result was a Senate Armed Services Committee's investigation into Marine Corps recruiting and recruit training. The Corps was in jeopardy of losing the right to make Marines. Recruit training is one of the things that gives the Corps its identity, so losing control of it could threaten the organization's existence. Fortunately, the training was allowed to remain in Marine hands, only because the Corps promised to improve the screening and training of drill instructors and to further increase officer supervision.

It wasn't until the early eighties that five graduation requirements were established to clarify the standards required to earn the title of Marine: rifle qualification, swim qualification, physical fitness test, 80 percent on academic tests, and battalion-commander's inspection. The quality of recruits began to rise as programs to fight drug use and racism became more successful. In 1987, Gen. Alfred Gray saw deficiencies in warfighting ability and created Basic Warrior Training (BWT). This contributed to the overwhelming success the Corps would experience in the near future. BWT included training with weapons organic to the Marine rifle squad, and basic tactics. It was another step to ensure that every Marine was a rifleman first.

The 1990s brought with it new challenges, for there was no longer the threat of war with the Soviet Union, meaning that the United States stood alone as the world's only superpower. With this distinction came additional responsibilities, which in turn led to the Corps finding itself busy in the Middle East, Africa, and many other places. The Marines now not only had to contend with enemy soldiers, but also with the phenomenon of "fighters," not tied to an identifiable force and intermixed with innocent civilians on a largely urban battlefield. Many operations required Marines to have new skills, so the Corps looked to its recruit training as one way to improve the force. In 1995, Gen. Carl E. Mundy (commandant 1991–1995) called on drill instructors to teach core values—honor, courage, and commitment—to provide recruits with the tools to identify clearly the differences between right and wrong. Its implementation was met with some reluctance, as some confused it with "sensitivity" training, but that soon disappeared and drill instructors embraced the core values as something they could use to make the Corps better.

Finally in 1996, the commandant Gen. Charles C. Krulak strengthened the transformation from civilian to Marine by directing the creation of a culminating training exercise. Where the other services looked for ways to lower the stress of entry-level training and make military service more attractive, the Marines continued to make it as tough as possible. He made it more realistic and challenging by using a defining moment that put the recruit-training experience into focus. General Krulak added an extra week to the training schedule and created yet another graduation requirement—*the Crucible!*

The Crucible is intended to continue the tradition of Marines being better warriors through shared hardship and teamwork. It creates an experience to demonstrate to each recruit the limitless possibilities of what they could achieve individually and how much more they could accomplish when working as a team. It was possibly the most dramatic change in the history of recruit training ever, but few would argue with the fact that it was a stroke of genius.

1

Reveille

The lights popped on silently, noticeably different from how they had come on for the past seventy-eight days. Usually, the rush of light through the eyelids would be accompanied by stringent sounds of reveille blasting over the base loudspeakers, and drill instructors yelling for the recruits to get out of the racks and to the position of attention. Their harsh voices were terror to ears enjoying a restful slumber just seconds before. The shock to the system increased the pulse rate and breathing of the recruits instantly, resulting in a platoon of wanna-be Marines standing at attention with slightly heaving chests seconds after the lights came on.

But today it was 0200, far too early to blast music over the loudspeakers, and the drill instructors didn't need to yell anymore. Even in the silence the recruits demonstrated a sense of urgency when they instinctively got on their feet and formed in their usual positions in front of their racks. For them, today was the beginning of the end. This reveille was welcomed like none before, because it marked the beginning of their final trek toward becoming United States Marines—the Crucible!

The Crucible Event is a fifty-four-hour endurance course in which recruits conquer challenge after challenge in increasingly demanding conditions. The continuous operations push the men beyond their own perceived limits and thus redefine the potential of their abilities. It features little food and sleep, plus forty miles of hiking. Most importantly, they must do everything as a team to be successful.

Each of the thirty-two combat exercises requires teamwork to be mastered; none can be accomplished alone. So the recruits were going to learn something important about not only themselves, but about each other and the value of teamwork. It would become obvious that each man had something to offer and was in some way valuable to the team. Where size and strength might be important at one station, it would be a liability at another that required agility and a small frame.

Eleven of the obstacles were named after Marine Medal of Honor[1] recipients, and a twelfth was named in honor of a Marine hero who sacrificed her life trying to save others from a fire in 1942. They were called warrior stations and served as the backbone of the Crucible. The course would be nothing but another endurance course if it were not for the emotional and spiritual effects of combining Marines' experiences from the past (Medal of Honor recipients), present (drill instructors), and future (recruits).

"Start getting dressed, Privates," yelped the senior drill instructor, Staff Sergeant Macias. He was a tall man with a powerful muscular frame that was complemented by his high and tight flattop haircut.

"Aye, aye, sir," fifty-two men screamed together. They were still standing at the position of attention, dressed only in white boxer shorts and green T-shirts. Directly behind them sat a footlocker that held all of their possessions, and behind it was the rack from which they'd just been roused. All was, of course, perfectly arranged. Meticulous attention to detail was placed on having a squared-away barracks where the platoon lived.

"What did I tell you last night, Privates?" asked Staff Sergeant Macias. He raised his voice, *"What did I say, Guide?"*

"To call the senior drill instructor by his rank . . . sir," answered the platoon guide, Private Bare. As the guide he was considered to be the best recruit in the platoon, an honor which, if he kept it for the next three days, would earn him a Marine Corps dress blue uniform to wear at graduation next week. The drill instructors, usually the senior drill instructor, made the selection of who would be the guide.

1. The Medal of Honor is our nation's highest and most respected award for valor. It was created by Congress in December 1861 and was first awarded to six soldiers in the Union Army on 25 March 1863.

"Good, Guide! You can't even do it yourself. Have I trained a bunch of nasty undisciplined privates? Well, have I?" he asked sarcastically, trying not to smile.

"No, Staff Sergeant," sounded off the platoon. For almost three months they called their senior drill instructor "sir." In fact, every Marine they spoke to received a sir or ma'am from the recruits. It was going to take some work before they were able to answer in any other way. The thought of being able to call a Marine by his or her rank seemed so far away. Doing it was difficult, especially when it was *their* senior drill instructor.

"You're going to be United States Marines in fifty-four hours, Privates, and I expect you to start getting the feeling now. I don't want you running around the Marine Corps calling enlisted men sir, so you better change your nasty ways. Shave and get ready to step off on our first hike. You've got less than thirty minutes before we move." He went into his office and shut the hatch. Even out of sight the platoon knew their senior drill instructor was smirking. As demanding and intimidating as he was, they recognized that he had a great sense of humor and was likely enjoying the platoon's inability to do something as simple as calling him by his rank. Probably he was even a little flattered that the change didn't come too easily for them.

Things were changing, changing fast. Private John Simms was uncertain whether this newness was something to be valued or dreaded. There was relative security in things remaining the same, even when the same meant that he was a United States Marine Corps recruit. All of the members of Platoon 3075 were called "recruit" for the first few months of boot camp, but after they qualified with their M16A2 service rifle Staff Sergeant Macias said they had earned the right to be called private. It was a huge confidence builder for Simms, making him prouder of his marksmanship badge than he was of any other award he ever received.

New privileges meant new responsibilities, however. In exchange for this title, Simms and his fellow recruits were expected to act more like Marines. But calling the drill instructors anything other than sir was something he would probably never get used to. It caused confusion similar to the first time one of his friends' parents told him to call them by their first names. That made him feel a little more

grown up, but he wasn't quite sure how this latest game of seman-
tics made him feel. He wanted to be a Marine, even though he was
still learning what being a Marine meant. At the very least, he now
knew there was a lot more to it than just wearing a uniform and carrying a rifle.

Simms probably enlisted for all the wrong reasons. After failing
to get into the colleges that he wanted, he was confused, questioning what to do with his life. He therefore decided to do something
totally out of character. His first impulse was to join the Army, but
once when he visited his Army recruiter, the Marine recruiter started
a conversation. By then, Simms had spoken with recruiters from all
the other services except the Marine Corps. Though he was unwilling to admit it, he was frightened of the Marines. They seemed too
far above his perceived ability for them to be a possibility, and the
last thing he wanted to do was fail at his first step into adulthood.
But the fear also lit a fire inside him that led to his being there, because it was part of his motivation to join. The Marines scared him
and he finally decided to take on his fear instead of hiding from it
as he had in the past.

In the presence of the recruiter, face to face, he found that he was
right in his perception that there was something different about the
Marines. There was nothing that he could really describe or put his
finger on, just that they were different. Where all of the other services offered him something—"Be all that you can be," "Join the adventure," "Aim high"—the Marine recruiter spoke of what he, John
Simms, was going to offer the Corps. MAYBE YOU CAN BE ONE OF US,
said the poster behind the sergeant's desk. Right from the beginning
there were questions about *his* qualifications: high-school grad, any
drug use, trouble with the law? There was an initial strength test that
he had to pass before he could even be sent to boot camp.

The whole process captivated Simms, because he had never felt
part of anything that he considered special. His parents were divorced when he was young, making family relationships awkward. As
hard as he tried, he was never anything other than average at sports
or in school. If he could just make it, he could see himself as part of
something special. Even if he were the worst one in the Corps, he
would still be a Marine and most others of his age group would never

be. Bottom line, Simms joined because the Marine Corps offered him something that he was going to have to earn. Nothing was free, as the recruiter told him.

Simms's parents had mixed reactions. His mother, after she realized that he was serious, said that she would prefer it if he went to college but that the Marines were lucky to get him. That made him feel great. His father laughed, telling him that he would never make it because he was too stubborn and hotheaded. That made him angry. Neither reaction was out of character for his parents. His mother always boosted his confidence, and his father was always a blow to it. So he prepared for boot camp with mixed motivations, not wanting to disappoint his mom, while also wanting to prove his father wrong.

Finally, the day came when his recruiter took him to the military entrance processing station that would get him on a plane headed for the Marine Corps Recruit Depot in San Diego. The screening at the center went smoothly, and Simms was soon on his way. The flight was far too short, and there was a Marine waiting to put Simms and the other recruits on a bus. Everyone was nervous with the bus from the airport reeking of the funky body odor young men produce when they are under stress.

When the bus pulled into the base, Simms was met with a rush of excitement and adrenaline. The Marine at the gate, dressed in a uniform consisting of a short-sleeve khaki shirt and green trousers, gave a crisp arm movement to signal the bus in. It all seemed like a movie, surreal in its appearance, and he wished his family and friends could see what he was doing. The elation was quickly crushed when a frightening character got on the bus and made it clear that they were to get off—*Now!*

Onto the sidewalk the busload of long-haired civilians jumped, meeting a storm of chaos caused by drill instructors who herded them into position. They stood on yellow footprints painted on the ground, forcing the men on the bus into a unit formation, their first step into a world of rigid organization and structure.

Simms looked to his left and right, only to have a drill instructor begin a savage verbal assault. He stood eyeball to eyeball and yelled a barrage of detailed instructions, making it clear to Simms that the only thing he should be doing is listening to the drill instructor at the front of the formation.

"YOU ARE NOW ONBOARD MARINE CORPS RECRUIT DEPOT, SAN DIEGO. FROM HERE ON OUT, THE FIRST OR THE LAST WORD OUT OF YOUR MOUTH WILL BE 'SIR.' YOU WILL NOT SPEAK WITHOUT ASKING PERMISSION TO DO SO FIRST. YOU WILL DO EXACTLY WHAT YOU'RE TOLD; WILLINGLY, INSTANTLY, AND WITHOUT QUESTION. ARE THERE ANY QUESTIONS?" There were, of course, none.

Simms reached up with his hand and scratched his cheek. An unconscious act motivated by a lifetime of conditioning to expect instant gratification. This time two drill instructors attacked. By the end of their tongue lashing, Simms was visibly shaken and nearly in tears.

Soon the new Marine recruits would lose their long hair and be dressed in a brand-new set of camouflage utilities. Their civilian clothing and belongings were packed and stored, no use to the recruits now.

The first few days were confusing, dizzying to the Corps' newest members. Everything was different from the way life as a normal eighteen-year-old kid was supposed to be. From one place to another: medical checks, administrative processing, classes, and more classes. Worst of all, the drill instructors were terrifying. Simms found himself doing anything and everything that prevented his bringing attention to himself and being singled out from the others. They struck absolute terror into him because their appearance and command presence were unrivaled.

Before Simms knew it he was on his third day and running another initial strength test. Surprisingly, he scored worse that he did for the recruiter. The shock to his body over the past few days, both physically and emotionally, obviously had taken a toll on his ability to perform.

All he had to do to pass was two pull-ups, forty-four crunches in two minutes, and a mile-and-a-half run in thirteen minutes and thirty seconds. To most the standards sounded achievable, but put the three together and many failed. For those who played football or wrestled, the pull-ups and sit-ups came easy, but the run seemed like a marathon. Men who ran cross-country or played basketball had the endurance to make the run easily, but lacked enough upper-body strength for the pull-ups and sometimes the sit-ups. For those who sat behind a computer all day or played baseball, the whole thing could be a living hell.

In the end, 5 to 10 percent would fail the initial strength test and therefore be dropped from the company before training started. They went to the physical conditioning platoon (PCP) where each would reach the minimum fitness level before joining a training company. It was a horrid thing to have this happen, for there was no graduation date or moving forward until minimum standards were achieved. Most would meet the requirements in about two weeks, but some would spend months in PCP before they passed.

With the completion of the strength test, the recruits were done with Receiving Company and the drill instructors with whom they had spent the past few days. The Receiving Company drill instructors were responsible for the reception and processing of a new group of recruits each week, after which they were transferred to a training company. Simms and the other recruits were now ready to become part of Company I, 3d Recruit Training Battalion, Recruit Training Regiment based on the Marine Corps Recruit Depot in San Diego. Simms would soon find that his new drill instructors would expect even more and seem even more terrifying.

A typical recruit platoon is made up of fifty to ninety recruits and was supervised by three to five drill instructors. Three or four platoons are combined to form a series led by an officer, usually a lieutenant or junior captain, and a chief drill instructor, usually a gunnery sergeant. Often, there is an additional officer who serves as an assistant series commander. Two series are combined to form a recruit training company led by a more senior captain and a first sergeant who is at least on his second tour of drill-instructor duty.

Simms quickly grew to hate boot camp. As far as he was concerned, he had made a terrible mistake that needed to be reversed. He thought about his parents, causing him to reconsider, but most of the time all he wanted was to be off the depot. Everything else seemed too far away. It was difficult for him to realize that if he did leave, there would still be a tomorrow. Within weeks, many who quit tried to reenter after realizing that the real mistake was leaving.

There is no freedom for a recruit, no opportunity to relax and do what he wants. Distractions like television, stereo, and telephones were all absent from recruit training. Every minute of the day is meticulously planned, with most days beginning at a 0530 reveille. Morning clean-up and chow came first, usually followed by some sort of physical fitness training. Physical fitness was important, as Vince Lombardi pointed out when he said, "Fatigue makes cowards of us all." The rest of each day is a hectic mix of classes and close-order drill. Classes cover a variety of subjects: history, close combat, weapons, first aid, and general military subjects.

Simms was told when and what to eat, where to be and when. He even had to ask permission to speak or use the head.[2] He had to learn a new vocabulary: a wall was a "bulkhead," the stairs were "ladder wells," the floor was a "deck," and the words "I," "me," or "my" didn't exist anymore.

"I, I, I! THERE IS NO 'I' IN 'TEAM,' SIMMS!" He was to refer to himself as "Recruit Simms" or "this recruit." Now speaking was stressful too, as a confusing tongue twister became required for every task.

"Sir, Recruit Simms requests permission to speak to senior drill instructor Staff Sergeant Macias." It wasn't an easy thing to do when trying to get the attention of a terrifying Marine wearing the drill-instructor campaign hat. Simms had to rehearse what he wanted to say in his head, making it into a conscious act rather than just babbling on as before.

"WHAT!?" they always yelled. It seemed that the drill instructors were incapable of talking in a normal conversational tone. Simms thought the drill instructors who processed him during his first few days were scary, but then he met those who would actually train him for three months. They seemed twice as intimidating as the others, making it even more difficult to speak.

"Sir, Recruit Simms requests permission to make a head call." He was a long way from getting up in the middle of a class at high school and leaving, knowing the teacher couldn't do anything. Here every action had a consequence, and a lack of action could, too. Some were good, others were bad, but everything required thought if one was

2. Head: Naval word for latrine or bathroom.

to be successful. Though he didn't know it yet, the same is true in combat.

All of the yelling, the "slinging stress" as Marines call it, was an important part of being a drill instructor. It wasn't that they were nasty, violent, and uncaring human beings. Actually, they were sensitive and loving spouses and parents when they weren't at work. The yelling and stress had a purpose.

Marine Corps boot camp and the drill instructor were often misunderstood entities. Contrary to popular civilian opinion, the drill instructors were not trying to break the recruits down. Instead, they were building them up by challenging them constantly. Nothing could ever be done fast enough or good enough, with the recruits always being driven to improve. Each recruit needs to rise to the occassion and meet the challenge, or fail and fall behind the group.

Anything could be turned into frustrating adversity, even making a rack in the morning: "You have sixty seconds to finish your racks," said the drill instructor. "Sixty, fifty-nine, fifty-eight, fifty-seven, forty-two, thirty-six, twenty, twelve, ten, nine, eight, seven, six, five, four, three, two, one, *ZERO!*"

"Freeze, Recruit, freeze," sounded the platoon, all now standing at rigid attention. Sixty seconds in drill instructor time actually equated to fifteen. The recruits were breathing heavily, winded in their attempt to accomplish an easy task which now seemed impossible.

"ZERO!"

"Freeze, Recruit, freeze."

"KEEP TAKING YOUR TIME! KEEP TAKING YOUR *FRIGGIN'* TIME. *TEAR THEM UP!* TEAR UP THE RACKS AND START OVER. Sixty, fifty-nine, fifty-eight . . ."

Drill instructors are hard on recruits because they must teach them to function in stressful environments. Some would say that they were trying to duplicate the stress of combat, usually individuals who never experienced its grim reality. No man's yelling could ever replace the stress and fear accompanying the artillery and gunfire of an enemy trying to kill.

The yelling was combined with meticulous attention to detail and constant corrections to pressure the recruit as much as possible. It created a stressful environment of constant chaos. The only certainty in combat was that it would be an uncertain and chaotic experience. Teaching recruits to operate in such an environment is essential to their performing the duties that would accomplish the future missions assigned to the Corps.

The stressful circumstances in which Simms and his fellow recruits were placed forced them to deal with the panicky feeling that was a natural part of being human. The fight-or-flight feeling is instinctive in all of us when faced with fearful circumstances and situations. When the air is exploding with gunfire, it's natural to want to flee, but a Marine must resist all natural impulses and fight instead. To a lesser degree, trying to lace up your boots with someone yelling in your face makes it hard for a recruit to control his natural instincts. He must control the panic so that even the small task at hand can be accomplished. This ability has saved many lives through the years when Marines have found themselves in positions of needing to clear jammed rifles before an enemy got in a position to kill them. While the recruits weren't aware of it, the stress was designed to increase as they became more Marine-like. Finally, it reached a point where they were completely comfortable, surviving and even thriving in a chaotic environment. Courage is not the absence of fear, it is the ability to overcome fear.

After little less than a week, at the five-day mark, Simms was about as close to quitting as he would come. He watched and plotted, trying to come up with a plan to get discharged without embarrassing himself. The best thing, he thought, would be if he were to be hurt one morning at physical training, nothing serious, but something that would put him on a plane home. His concern with that was the possibility that he would only be hurt badly enough to be sent to the medical rehabilitation platoon (MRP). This was another nightmare away from the training routine that put a recruit in limbo without a scheduled graduation date. A rumor was circulating of recruits spending as long as six months recovering in MRP.

He thought of becoming a disciplinary problem, perhaps faking a suicide, or climbing over the fence and going UA (unauthorized absence). The thought of legal ramifications entered his mind, but he knew that it wouldn't be that great a blow to his future. He knew that too many powerful people had avoided military service for it to be that serious a black mark. If he weren't so scared, trying one of the three might already have happened, but for now he only plotted. One thing he'd learned thus far was that actions had consequences.

That same day, when he was at his lowest, was also the day that a seed was planted, making him believe that maybe he could make it. His series commander, 1st Lieutenant Harris, was giving a class about core values: honor, courage, and commitment. The lieutenant made it clear from his behavior that there was something different between officers and enlisted men. He first sent the drill instructors out of the classroom for a break. He told the recruits that he was going to treat them like Marines, and if they acted like Marines he would stay to teach. If they were to act like recruits, he would leave and let the drill instructors deal with their behavior. It was easy to decide which alternative was preferable, so the lieutenant stayed and taught.

"So who's ready to quit?" he asked. "Too afraid to even raise your hands, huh? Let me just tell you that the feeling you're having, this doubt you have in yourself is nothing different from what all of your fellow recruits are feeling." Simms felt as if the lieutenant was ignoring the other 187 recruits and speaking only to him. "Even your drill instructors felt this same way; you know that? Let me tell you about Recruit Harris who was sitting here about ten years ago. That's right; I was a recruit myself. And there was one day, a little behind where you are now, the second training day, I think it was, that I knew I had made a mistake. I was ready to do anything to get out of here. There was even one point when I was on firewatch about zero dark thirty on the third deck of a squad bay feeling sorry for myself. Out of one side of the squad bay I could see the planes taking off from the airport, thinking about how they were going someplace away from here. Out the other side I could see the fireworks from Sea World, reminding me of all the fun I could be having somewhere else. I was done, I knew it, and I decided that when the lights came on in the morning I was going to do something to get me thrown out of here. I was going to go home. I was going to quit. Well, obviously, I didn't quit, did I? I wouldn't be here if I had, right? Anyone think they know why I didn't?"

"Sir, the series commander found the strength to live up to his commitment," one recruit said.

"No," said Lieutenant Harris as he motioned for the recruit to sit back down.

"Sir, the series commander thought about how his family would feel if he failed," said another, again, who was told to sit down because his answer was wrong.

"Recruits, I've got no stinking idea why," said 1st Lieutenant Harris sarcastically, causing the recruits to lose their composure and smile, even laugh. "As much as I would like to say that I dug deep within myself and that I found the strength, for some other reason, I didn't quit. Now ten years later I'm a Marine Corps officer and you are here . . . think about it. Each one of you is ten years away from being an officer yourself. Or better yet, ten years away from being a senior drill instructor. Or maybe even ten years away from being a successful civilian who honorably served four years in the Corps. Or you're ten years away from being another guy sitting next to me at the airport saying, 'I almost was a Marine.' I can't tell you how many times I've heard that, and there's always a sad story to go along with the reason they didn't make it.

"Don't think in terms of days, months, or even years, Recruits. Think about how the next three months will impact your entire life. Don't quit! Don't ever quit! Be certain that if you do," he paused and scanned the classroom to add dramatic effect, "it will only make your drill instructors' job harder. They're Marines and you're not going to see them quit. They don't know how anymore, so even when you quit on yourself they're still going to train you. They're still going to push you. If you get sent to see me, I'm just going to give you a little motivation talk and send you right back to train. Ten years isn't that far away. Trust me, I know. We can't be wasting time with you in my office crying when there's training to be done."

The last comment left his lips just as the lieutenant was out of the direct sight of the recruits in the back row of the classroom. There was a pause as he reached the back door to let the drill instructors back in. Like the pop of a pressurized cabin, the opening of the classroom door caused an eruption of chaos and turbulence that immediately changed the environment. The cozy atmosphere that the lieutenant intentionally had created among the recruits was shattered by the drill instructors who came in yelling for the recruits to get out.

The suddenly altered situation was designed to keep the recruits experiencing many changes. One day they could find themselves reacting to confusing changes of environment in a short period of time. They might feed the hungry one minute and be engaging a deadly enemy with rifle fire the next. Humans, being creatures of habit, find it easy to lapse into a setting of comfort that could be dangerous during an operation. If the enemy were to shock or surprise them out of that coziness, their lives would depend on their ability to adapt quickly to the changing situation.

The day after Lieutenant Harris's story, Simms was assigned as squad leader, making him even more happy that he hadn't quit. He was actually doing better than he thought, and his constant desire to do everything quickly so the drill instructors wouldn't yell at him made them think that he was motivated. His drill instructors made it clear by telling Simms that it wasn't so much that he was squared away, as that the rest of the recruits were even more nasty. Drill instructors had a hilarious talent for explaining things that way. A compliment took the form of an insult to others rather than a favorable comment about the individual. Simms knew they were joking though, so he was very proud of his billet. It meant that the drill-instructor team thought he was the best recruit in the squad and one of the best in the platoon.

The first few weeks of training were probably the worst, but not because the schedule was the most challenging; it would get much worse, but the men were still learning how to become Marine Corps recruits. The new culture in which they were now immersed was a shock to their systems, so it was difficult to keep them focused and motivated. Because of this, all the drill instructors were present every day including Sundays. They would be there when the lights came on at 0530 and still there when they went out again at 2130.

It seemed like a long experience for the recruits, but seemed even longer for the drill instructors. The recruit training cycle is twelve weeks, broken into several different parts, processing, first phase, second phase, and a transition week. Processing occurred in the receiving company and covered only a few days.

The first phase takes place at MCRD, San Diego, for seven weeks. It includes basic military skills, physical conditioning, swim training, close order drill, history, core values, and mess or maintenance duty. The purpose of this phase is to transition the civilian into a recruit.

The second phase takes place at Camp Pendleton, forty miles north of San Diego. It is a four-week period of training on marksmanship and weapons, field skills, and core values, culminating with the Crucible. Its purpose is to transform the recruit into a basic Marine.

The final week of training is back at MCRD, San Diego, and introduces the new Marines to life in the Corps. It is intended to transition them from the strict regimen of recruit training to an environment of professionalism and self-discipline that Marines are expected to exhibit in the Fleet Marine Force. The week climaxes with a graduation parade for friends and family on Friday morning.

Simms was a little more than a week away from graduation now, and through all the challenges of the past eleven weeks he was still a squad leader. If he kept his billet during the Crucible, it would lead to a meritorious promotion to private first class, a great way to earn that first stripe.

"Is the squad ready, Simms?" asked drill instructor Sergeant Lee, obviously the most junior member of the four drill instructors. He was not junior in rank or time in the Marine Corps, but in terms of experience as a drill instructor. They were all exceptional Marines, the finest the Corps could offer. Making Marines was a learned skill, however, so experience gave a drill instructor an advantage. Being the least experienced meant that Lee was still learning, himself. Senior drill instructor Staff Sergeant Macias was responsible for supervising the team. He personally taught many of the core values classes by leading guided discussions with the platoon. Drill instructor Staff Sergeant Washington, called the "strong-J," conducted close-order drill. Drill instructor Sergeant McLeary, called the "third hat," retaught all of the classes that the recruits had already received from the depot's academic instruction unit. Sergeant Lee helped the others, or filled in during their absence, but he seemed to have a special liking for having the recruits perform push-ups. They were beginning to wonder if he was secretly responsible for getting the platoon in perfect physical condition.

"I don't know, sir," answered Simms after turning around and coming to the position of attention.

"What did the senior drill instructor tell you?"

"I don't know, Sergeant," he corrected himself. To Simms, Sergeant Lee was as impressive as a human being could be. He was not a large man, only five feet five, but he had a command presence that made him seem ten feet tall. It was obvious by the number of awards he wore on his service uniform that his combat record was extraordinary. It wasn't until the senior drill instructor told the platoon about his exploits that the recruits really learned of his past.

An infantryman, or "grunt," by trade, Sergeant Lee's first award for heroism came as a young Marine during Desert Storm. He went into a live minefield to help an engineer who had been hurt trying to set a breaching charge. Without hesitation, he went to the aid of his brother Marine, carrying him under his small frame to a medical aid station. This was the kind of stuff movies were made of, and here he was in front of Simms.

Although the senior drill instructor didn't go into the same detail with Sergeant Lee's other adventures, Simms knew that he also served in Somalia. Most impressively Lee didn't brag about his service. There were some who tried to play up any combat experience they might have, telling elaborate war stories about minor incidents. They failed to realize that the recruits could see through a yahoo story quicker than a Marine can state the name of the only Marine to receive five Navy Crosses—*Chesty Puller.*

"You're the squad leader; you need to go check on your men. Make sure they're getting shaved and ready, cause we'll be leaving in about ten minutes," said Sergeant Lee. He couldn't blame Simms for forgetting to call him by rank. It was going to take him a while to get used to it. Such things were absolutely unheard of when Lee went through recruit training, but some things are different nowadays.

Exiting the barracks into the early Southern California air, Sergeant Lee nearly ran right into Lieutenant Harris. "Good morning, sir," he said, trying to render a proper salute, but not quite getting his right hand to the brim of his camouflage utility hat, known in Marine lingo as a "cover."

"Not going to get used to that thing again, are you?" laughed the lieutenant. He was referring to the utility cover, because the drill instructors normally wore their huge campaign cover called a "Smokey." Each drill instructor cherished his Smokey. The large circular rim protected the face and neck from the punishment of the sun, making it a favorite of Marines serving in combat in Haiti, Nicaragua, and France during the early 1900s.

"No, sir," chuckled Sergeant Lee, "I never realized how small this thing is," pointing to his utility cover.

Not using the campaign cover during the fifty-four hours was another difference from when Lee was a recruit. Then, the drill instructors always had them on, but now the Crucible required that they be put away for a few days. It was considered to be an important part of reinforcement to the recruits that they were now different, that they were about to become Marines. It sounded simple, but really was a complicated process. For a recruit to be allowed to call himself "private," to be allowed to call his drill instructor by his rank, to see that his drill instructor wore the same uniform as he, all helped to transform him into a Marine. But these tangible things were the easy stuff. The real challenge was in the change of relationship between the recruit and drill instructor. Recruits could do many new things, but nothing would make these young men believe that they were different until they realized that the drill instructors were treating them differently. For a drill instructor to stop a recruit from saying "sir," and tell him that he would have to act like a Marine soon, reinforced the purpose behind the Crucible. It strengthened the commitment that the recruits must have to Corps and country, highlighting the personal responsibility that came with the title "Marine."

Even though the Crucible was tough, it was also intended to reinforce core values. It was one response to many of the problems the Corps was having with Marine conduct both in and out of uniform. The recruits' core-values training began early in the first week with Lieutenant Harris's class and would continue as long as they wore the Marine uniform.

Recruits don't have defective value systems, but some are deficient in their ability to distinguish between right and wrong. It is debatable whether this is anything new to American society. Marines from generations past were not that much different from the men and women joining today. The problem is that a Marine's misbehavior in a foreign country is more apt today to cause an international incident. As an expeditionary force spending much of its time deployed on Navy vessels, there are opportunities for Marines to jeopardize American influence in a region. The purpose of core values is to make Marines better warriors by making them better Americans, causing units in turn to be more effective.

At each warrior station the drill instructor reads the Medal of Honor citation for the Marine the event was named after. The citations are then used during debriefs after the event to relate the actions of the recruits to core values. The drill instructors use every opportunity to discuss honor, courage, and commitment. They point out incidents that make the recruits realize how core values can make a unit better.

"Get over here, fourth squad," barked Sergeant Lee as the recruits exited the squad bay. It was now 0226, and in the past half hour the recruits had washed and shaved with the last drop of hot water they would experience until they were full-fledged Marines. Their camouflage packs each weighed more than forty pounds, adding to their load-bearing vests with cartridge belt, ammunition pouches, and canteens. The packs were full of equipment and uniforms, plus the small amount of food they would eat during the Crucible.

Food deprivation is a terrifying word for anyone who has experienced harsh training environments. There is no enjoyment in carrying a heavy load mile after mile, but it is a completely different experience without proper nutrition. The psychological effects of having a rumbling stomach, but knowing that there is no possibility of food, is shattering to morale. The recruits of India Company, Platoon 3075, like all recruits on the Crucible, would only get two and one-half meals to eat during the fifty-four-hour event. The meals were MREs (meals ready to eat), rations packaged in thick plastic bags. The food was bland and often freeze-dried, but it was better than nothing.

Why two and one-half? Many with a purpose in mind asked this when the Crucible was to begin. *What is half an MRE?* Splitting an MRE would cause the recruits to use teamwork before they left the barracks, because two recruits would have to share one meal. Most would take turns picking what they wanted from the ration, while others sacrificed from the beginning by giving their buddies with larger frames the majority of the meal. Regardless of the method, the message was clear: *We're in this together.*

"The squad is ready, Sergeant," Simms said confidently.

"Outstanding," answered Sergeant Lee, feeling somewhat different about the recruit who was now calling him "sergeant" instead of "sir." "Line them up so I can do a quick check of their gear."

"Aye, aye, Sergeant."

The Corps' story is one of survival, and good Marines always adapt, improvise, and overcome when they meet challenging situations. That's the way it always has been, but change does not come easily. The Crucible was one of the biggest changes on how recruit training has been conducted for the previous eighty-five years, but it was not a response to a Marine Corps boot camp in disrepair. Instead, it came from changes in both the operations required of Marines and the subtle societal shifts that had happened to America's youth. Because the Corps has little or no control over the two, they needed to adapt that which they could control—recruit training, the vital link between the recruiting office and the battlefield of tomorrow.

There were complaints from some that the Corps was lowering its standards and changing its methods to meet a generation of Americans viewed as weaker than those from the past. These complaints were from people who knew little about the Crucible. Those who insist on focusing entirely on the past will probably fail. One can't move forward very well while fixating on the past, because what worked yesterday may not work today or prepare us for tomorrow. The Corps was never able to simply accept young men and women off the streets and call them Marines. From the beginning, with the use of the rookie squads, some form of recruit training was always necessary and was always changing. Every generation seems to think that the next is misguided and less capable. This is a strange phenomenon, but especially true for Marines, who when they graduate look at the new recruits and comment on how it was back when they joined, just *three* months earlier. The "old Corps" was always better, but the definition was related to whom you were talking, not a specific date in history.

Few in the squad actually possessed all of the traits needed to be a good Marine, but the Crucible would help them develop more. Pulled from the streets and high schools across the country, they were about as diverse a group as could be mustered in any organization. In any other segment of society they would probably never be found together. Their backgrounds, family lives, and education all differed to some degree, but they all had one underlying commonality—*they wanted to be Marines!*

Simms was clearly the best, chosen as the squad leader, but he too had some weaknesses. He often became frustrated by failure and couldn't seem to vary his methods for motivating the other recruits. Quick to yell, a skill he learned from the drill instructors, he didn't yet see that shouting wouldn't always work. He would learn on the Crucible or suffer enormous frustration; he might even fail. Many squad members respected him as their leader, but Sergeant Lee sensed that some thought poorly of him, a not uncommon situation when peers are placed in a position superior to one another. He thought Simms clearly didn't have much male influence in his upbringing and could be classified as a "momma's boy." He practically worshipped the drill instructors, hanging on their every word because they gave him something that he lacked by growing up with a father who lived outside of the house and worked too much.

"This is the plan, fourth squad," said Sergeant Lee. Even without shouting, he still shook the silent night. "We're going to hike up to the bivouac site, a little over a mile away, and set up the hootches. From there we go on another little hike and about five miles later we'll be at our first station." It was 0253 and there was only a little more than fifty-three hours to go. "Saddle up!"

2

Staff Sergeant Howard's Maze

Americans first became involved in Vietnam during World War II, when the U.S. Office of Special Services (OSS) helped Ho Chi Minh's guerrillas fight the Japanese. In return, Ho helped rescue downed American air crews and collected intelligence about the Japanese military. After the war, France became locked in a bitter struggle for power with Ho, and the American support shifted away from the communist guerrillas.

France's Indochina War practically ended in mid-1954 with the surrender of the French garrison at Dien Bien Phu. Up to that point, the U.S. Military Assistance and Advisory Group (MAAG) was concerned primarily with providing logistical support to the French forces. Now, with the French unable to continue, the MAAG began to focus on organizing, training, and equipping the South Vietnamese forces. Lieutenant Colonel Victor J. Croizat soon found himself serving as the senior advisor to the small Vietnamese Marine Corps, and the U.S. Marine Corps began what would become twenty years of involvement in Vietnam.

Marine air units arrived in Vietnam to fly support operations for the Vietnamese in 1962. In April 1963, a small detachment of Marine infantry was sent to Da Nang to help provide security. The Gulf of Tonkin incident, in August 1964, led to Operation Rolling Thunder, a large air campaign against North Vietnam. The expanded role in the air increased the need for security on the ground, and on 8 March 1965, the 9th Marine Expeditionary Brigade[1] hit the beaches of Vietnam.

1. The Marine Expeditionary Brigade was soon renamed Marine Amphibious Brigade, because Gen. William Westmoreland of the Army was concerned that "expeditionary" sounded too French.

The Marine force grew rapidly: from 5,000 in April to more than 25,000 by summer's end. Even with these numbers, there were few large operations. Most Marines were participating in small patrols. Marine generals Victor Krulak (commanding general, Fleet Marine Force, Pacific) and Lewis Walt (commanding general, III Marine Amphibious Force), designed an enclave campaign plan that was referred to as a "spreading ink blot" pacification system. Such a strategy would take more time than the Army's "search-and-destroy" strategy, but it also reduced the likelihood of American casualties.

Civil action combined with interdiction operations, and in early 1966 Marines joined with Vietnamese forces to create Combined Action Platoons and Combined Action Companies.[2] To support these combined forces Marines conducted a series of operations to eradicate guerrillas. A common practice involved the placement of Marines in positions where they could observe large areas and use aircraft or artillery fires to destroy the enemy.

The Vietnam War was a sergeant-and-lieutenant's conflict, in which small unit leaders had to be independent. On 13 June 1965, helicopters landed a small Marine force in a position to observe much of the Que Son Valley in central South Vietnam. For the next two days they regularly called in fire missions on the enemy. To prevent the North Vietnamese from becoming suspicious of too many strikes, possibly leading them to think there might be Americans in the vicinity, some missions were denied. As the operation grew longer, most missions were reserved for times when an aircraft was in the air nearby, to lead the enemy to think they were being observed by aircraft, not infantrymen.

The overall commander was concerned about leaving the Marines in the field much longer and wanted to pull them out. The thirty-five-year-old former drill instructor leading the patrol protested, however, wanting to continue. It was decided to leave them in the field

2. Combined units were designed to increase the ability of local militia units to defend their own villages. The militias were reinforced with Marines who lived, worked, and fought with their Vietnamese counterparts.

for at least one more day, but, unfortunately, the enemy had learned the whereabouts of the Marines.

"This obstacle is named in honor of Jimmie E. Howard," said Sergeant Lee. It was 0600, the Crucible was only four hours old, and the recruits already had hiked more than six miles. "He was born in Burlington, Iowa, on 27 July 1929, and enlisted in the Marine Corps in July 1950. He served as a forward observer in Korea and was awarded the Silver Star and two Purple Hearts. The Silver Star is our third highest award for valor, and the Purple Hearts were awarded for wounds he received in combat. He earned the Medal of Honor in Vietnam.

The President of the United States in the name of The Congress takes pleasure in presenting the Medal of Honor to Gunnery Sergeant Jimmie E. Howard, United States Marine Corps, for service set forth in the following citation:

> For conspicuous gallantry and intrepidity at the risk of his life above and beyond the call of duty. Gunnery Sergeant Jimmie E. Howard and his eighteen-man platoon were occupying an observation post deep within enemy-controlled territory. Shortly after midnight a Vietcong force of estimated battalion size approached the Marines' position and launched a vicious attack with small arms, automatic weapons, and mortar fire. Reacting swiftly and fearlessly in the face of overwhelming odds, Gunnery Sergeant Howard skillfully organized his small but determined force into a tight perimeter defense and calmly moved from position to position to direct his men's fire. Throughout the night, during assault after assault, his courageous example and firm leadership inspired and motivated his men to withstand the unrelenting fury of the hostile fire in the seemingly hopeless situation. He constantly shouted encouragement to his men and exhibited imagination and resourcefulness in directing their return fire. When fragments of an exploding enemy grenade wounded him severely and prevented him from moving his legs, he distributed his ammunition to the remaining members of his platoon and proceeded to maintain radio communications and direct air strikes on the enemy with

uncanny accuracy. At dawn, despite the fact that five men were killed and all but one wounded, his beleaguered platoon was still in command of its position. When evacuation helicopters approached his position, Gunnery Sergeant Howard warned them away and called for additional air strikes and directed devastating small-arms fire and air strikes against enemy automatic weapons positions in order to make the landing zone as secure as possible. Through his extraordinary courage and resolute fighting spirit, Gunnery Sergeant Howard was largely responsible for preventing the loss of his entire platoon. His valiant leadership and courageous fighting spirit served to inspire the men of his platoon to heroic endeavor in the face of overwhelming odds, and reflect the highest credit upon Gunnery Sergeant Howard, the Marine Corps, and the U.S. Naval service. Signed, Lyndon B. Johnson[3]

The recruits were quiet. The citation was stirring and this was a good warrior station for them to begin their final trek toward becoming Marines. In front of the squad sat a spider web constructed of quarter-inch ropes suspended from a log frame.

"You're the leader for this one, Simms," said Sergeant Lee, "so listen up. Your squad is observing enemy movement from the basement of an abandoned building. An enemy observer discovers your squad and calls in artillery fire on your position. The building collapses around you, but you suffer no casualties. The only route of escape is through a mangled array of ventilation ducts." Sergeant Lee turned and pointed to the rope web. There were several different openings of different sizes. "You notice, however, that any movement through the openings causes loose debris and rubble to collapse in on that particular hole. Your mission is to evacuate your team and all of your equipment from the collapsed building before the enemy arrives. You will not wear any gear or sling your M16A2 service rifle, but your gear and rifle must go through the spaces in the web.

"Coordinating instructions: One, neither you nor your equipment may touch the web. If the web is touched the entire team begins

3. Medal of Honor citation from *The Congressional Medal of Honor, The Names, The Deeds* (Chico, Calif., Sharp and Dunnigan, 1988) 256.

again. Two, if a recruit is lifted through the obstacle, he must go feet first through the web. Three, once a hole in the obstacle has been used it will be marked and not used again. Before you take any action, you must brief me on your plan. Are there any questions?"

Simms organized the squad and asked for suggestions, but the other recruits didn't have much advice to offer. Because this was their first station, they weren't really clear on what they should do. Simms briefed Sergeant Lee on his plan, and the recruits got to work. Simms identified that the two holes closest to the ground provided the easiest route, and therefore they should be reserved for the first and the last recruit through.

He sent one of the larger recruits through the web first because his upper body strength would be useful in getting recruits through the higher holes in the web. The next recruit was lifted into a hole and carefully pushed through to the first recruit on the other side.

"STOP!" said Sergeant Lee, "look at the web." It was shaking slightly, indicating that someone had touched it. The ropes were stretched tight so it was impossible to touch them without everyone knowing. "Everyone back on this side and start over."

The squad made several attempts, only to start over when someone accidentally touched the web. At one point they got everyone through but one. Regrettably, he was not coordinated enough to get himself into the last hole so the others could pull him through. They had to start over yet again.

As they continued to try, the squad discovered that their mission could be accomplished only when they accepted that they needed to rely on each other. The man being passed through the web could not move his legs or arms without being told it was okay by another recruit. Not being able to see the complete web, each needed to trust that the squad would take care of him.

Finally, after more than twenty minutes of trying, Simms got the entire squad through to complete the event successfully. There were obvious mixed feelings in the squad. Some were pleased that finally they were successful while others were frustrated that they hadn't done it on the first try.

"You did pretty good," said Sergeant Lee. He had the recruits sit in a semicircle around him. "Before we start the debrief, I want to tell you more about Staff Sergeant Howard and his Marines. Two of his Marines were killed in the initial North Vietnamese assault. One fired his rifle till it ran out of ammo and then he used it as a club, killing two more enemy before they killed him. Another was wounded, but he killed two with his knife before he died. The fight was on, and the Marines weren't going to make it easy on the North Vietnamese.

"The sixteen remaining Marines formed a tight perimeter and threw back assault after assault. Howard continued to direct the defense of the hill even after being severely wounded. He distributed his ammunition to his Marines and painfully crawled from position to position, motivating his men and dragging a radio to direct artillery fire and air strikes. By the time a relief force reached their position, the Marines had eight rounds of ammunition left. Everyone was wounded and six were dead, but the surviving twelve were still fighting. They were firing single shots at the enemy and throwing rocks."

"Did he die, Sergeant?" asked a recruit.

"No, no," said Sergeant Lee, shaking his head. "He retired as a first sergeant and died of natural causes in November of 1993. So, Simms, tell me how you thought things went."

"It was a lot harder than I thought, Sergeant," said Simms. "I was expecting to be able to finish it on the first try."

"So when you were still failing on about the *seventeenth* try, how did it feel?" asked Sergeant Lee.

"Frustrating," said Simms.

"Anyone else feel that way?" asked Sergeant Lee.

"Yes, Sergeant, there were a couple of times when I didn't think it could be completed," said one recruit.

"Impossible odds?" Several of the men nodded in agreement. "So why didn't you just quit if there didn't seem to be a right answer?"

"We couldn't quit," said another recruit.

"Even though we kept experiencing failure," said Simms, "we were learning from our mistakes. We were getting better."

"And that's an important part of this," said Sergeant Lee. "You started working better as a team. By the time you were done you knew that the person being sent through the maze had little personal control over success or failure, right?"

"He had to remain still and trust that the others would put him through safely," said one of the recruits. "We needed to trust that someone else would watch our back 'cause we couldn't watch our own."

"Sixteen guys were stuck on a hill, surrounded with no hope of being rescued anytime soon. They were out of ammunition and wounded, but they didn't quit and they didn't surrender. What core value describes this action?"

"Courage is one, Sergeant," said a recruit. The squad had spent much of their past three months learning about core values.

Courage is the heart of core values. It is composed of mental, moral, and physical strength that are ingrained in all Marines to carry them through the challenges of combat and allow them to master their fears. It will help them to do what is right by adhering to a high standard of personal conduct, leading by example, and making tough decisions under stress and pressure.

"They demonstrated the inner strength that enables Marines to take that extra step," said another recruit.

"Understand that this is only one example of Marines demonstrating that type of behavior. You might even experience it in the very near future for yourself. I saw it in the Gulf War shortly after I graduated from recruit training.

"When Iraq invaded Kuwait on 2 August 1990, President Bush committed the United States to protect Saudi Arabia and liberate Kuwait. My unit immediately flew from the United States to Saudi Arabia, where we met MPS[4] equipment and got ready for war. Within six weeks there were 45,000 Marines in the region and by the time the ground war began we had 92,990, making it the largest single combat operation in history for the Marine Corps.

"On the first day of the ground war, a corporal named Kilpatrick and another Marine were returning to their base through the fog

4. Desert Shield/Storm was the first large test of the Corps' Maritime Pre-positioning Ship (MPS) doctrine. MPS ships are packed with the vehicles, weapons, and supplies Marines need to fight. Positioned in several locations throughout the world, the ships are sent to crisis areas to allow an immediate response to aggression. Marines are flown from the United States or Okinawa to meet the ships and draw the equipment, reducing the travel time necessary if the force had to depart the United States by ship.

and smoke. They'd been out directing air strikes against the enemy and suddenly encountered two enemy tanks and about twenty-five Iraqi soldiers. Being severely outnumbered and with limited firepower at their disposal, the two did what any good Marine would do—they demanded that the enemy surrender. Unfortunately for the enemy, they refused and fired on the Marines. The two Marines warned a nearby command post of the Iraqi counterattack, and later, Kilpatrick advanced through the fog and machine-gun fire to destroy a tank with an antitank missile."

On 2 July 1991, Corporal Kilpatrick would leave the Silver Star awarded him at the base of the Vietnam Memorial in Washington, D.C. Etched in black marble was the name of his father, Capt. Donald Kilpatrick, a helicopter pilot killed on 2 September 1969, while evacuating men near the Cambodian border. To Kilpatrick, his father deserved the medal more than he did.

"What's the significance of Marines like Kilpatrick and Howard?" asked Sergeant Lee.

"They fought hard," said Simms.

"They didn't surrender when it probably seemed like the only thing they could do," said a recruit.

"Especially with Gunnery Sergeant Howard," said another recruit, "the Marines hung in there and fought on against impossible odds."

"Kilpatrick actually expected the larger force to surrender, and when they didn't he went and warned a nearby unit of the Iraqis," said Sergeant Lee. "Are we talking about moral or physical courage here?"

"Both, Sergeant," said Simms.

"Did you have to show any courage?"

"Not really. Maybe a little moral courage by being the leader and making decisions."

"Did this obstacle require any physical stamina or endurance?" asked Sergeant Lee.

"No, Sergeant," said a recruit, "not really."

"What about in making decisions? Does being tired after getting up at zero-two and hiking all morning affect your ability to make decisions, Simms?"

"A little, I guess, Sergeant," answered Simms.

"Well it does, but we're still pretty fresh," Sergeant Lee said. "In a few hours this one here could have blown a brain cell or two because you would have been more tired. Being in shape helps you out. Three months ago when you showed up all out of shape and nasty, this would have been a different story, huh?"

The recruits chuckled and nodded in agreement. They were in much better shape now, and hadn't really noticed the effects of their already demanding day. Though this obstacle did not seem to require physical strength, endurance played an important role in it being successfully accomplished. Fatigue affects decision making and increases the likelihood of mistakes.

The recruit physical training program is well balanced and uses a "ramp-up" philosophy. Preventing injury is a priority, for the recruits could not train if they were hurt. Therefore, the distance of runs and demands of physical training sessions begins with the assumption that each recruit has barely passed the initial strength test. It then progresses to the point where most recruits can run at an eight-minute-mile pace for three miles. Many improve to run under seven-minute miles, and some break the coveted six-minute pace.

The recruits participate in many runs and exercise courses as part of their training. The obstacle course helps develop coordination, and the circuit course requires them to lift weights to increase muscular strength. The strength and endurance course combines both into one grueling event. At the end, to graduate, each recruit is required to pass the Marine Corps Physical Fitness Test (PFT).

The PFT is similar to the initial strength test, but the requirements are higher. For Marines, minimum standards are insignificant and all strive to obtain the maximum score. To get a perfect score of 300 on the PFT a recruit needs twenty dead-hang pull-ups, 100 crunches in two minutes, and a three-mile run in less than eighteen minutes.

It was already 0630 so the recruits had to move to the next warrior station. They had a decent start, but still had more than forty-nine hours left until they could claim the title "Marine."

3

Corporal Mackie's Passage

A telegram addressed to Lt. Col. Robert E. Lee, of the Army, ordered him to move immediately to the federal arsenal at Harpers Ferry. It was 17 October 1859, and a crusader named John Brown had seized the arsenal, killing several people, and taking thirteen hostages. A cavalry lieutenant named J. E. B. Stuart volunteered to accompany Lee as his aide; and the two were soon on their way.

There were no federal troops available, so eighty-five Marines from the Washington Barracks were sent with orders to report to the senior army officer on the scene. The Marine officer of the day, Lt. Israel Greene, grabbed his ceremonial sword and led the Marines to the train station for their trip north.

Upon reporting to Lee, Greene was instructed to divide his force into two storming parties. Stuart would try to negotiate a surrender, but would send a signal if it became obvious that force was necessary. Lee told the Marines not to risk a stray bullet killing a prisoner, and instead to use their bayonets.

Stuart went forward, the signal was seen, and the Marines attacked. Lieutenant Greene was the first man through the door; the number two and three men through were hit by gunfire. Seeing a bearded man on his knee reloading, Greene struck him in the back of the neck with his sword. The blow wounded John Brown, but the light ceremonial sword bent double before it could deliver a deadly blow. John Brown would live to stand trial, and the two wounded Marines became the first casualties of what would become the Civil War. Before it ended, more than 600,000 Americans would perish. An Irish-born Marine named Luke Quinn was just the first.

As the Civil War broke out, Marines were forced to choose between North and South. Some served in the new Confederate Marine Corps, but most stayed with the Union. Unfortunately, the Marines did not have a large role during the war so they found themselves serving in small detachments as gun crews and boarding parties. At war's end, the failure to demonstrate a vital wartime function would threaten the life of the Corps. Even with the small role, seventeen would earn the Medal of Honor, with the first being from the ironclad USS *Galena.*

"This obstacle is named in honor of John F. Mackie. Born in 1835 in New York, he joined the Marine Corps on 23 August 1861 and earned the Medal of Honor during the Civil War." It was 0635 and the recruits were still motivated. The 0200 reveille and morning hike was no match for the adrenaline from the completion of their first warrior station.

Citation: On board the U.S.S. *Galena* in the attack on Fort Darling at Drewry's Bluff, James River, on 15 May 1862. As enemy shellfire raked the deck of his ship, Corporal Mackie fearlessly maintained his musket fire against the rifle pits along the shore, and when ordered to fill vacancies at guns caused by men wounded and killed in action, manned the weapon with skill and courage.[1]

The recruits didn't really know what to think of the citation. It was short and not nearly as descriptive as the one for Staff Sergeant Howard. At the time it was written there was little need for verbose award recommendations, as commanders simply recommended brave warriors, and they received the awards.

"Drewry's Bluff sits eight miles below Richmond and rises two hundred feet above the James River. The river was obstructed by sunken vessels and Fort Darling was a heavily fortified position with a battery of ten guns," Sergeant Lee explained. He would go on to tell

1. Medal of Honor citation from *The Congressional Medal of Honor, The Names, The Deeds* (Chico, Calif., Sharp and Dunnigan, 1988) 840.

the recruits of how the twelve Marines of the ship's detachment
served as snipers shooting at the enemy. The USS *Galena* would be
hit more than a hundred times, with the deck of the ship being
pierced in twenty places. Of 150 crew members, sixty were killed or
wounded.

President Lincoln inspected the ship after the battle and com-
mented on how remarkable it was that anyone survived at all. When
three of the crew, including Corporal Mackie, were brought before
him as the "young heroes of the Fort Darling battle," he took them
by the hand and personally thanked each one. He also ordered that
their heroism be recognized with the Medal of Honor.

"Who wants to be the leader this time?" asked Sergeant Lee. A recruit named Nushi raised his hand. "Good, Nushi, you're the man
for this obstacle. Your squad is aboard a ship that has been struck by
enemy fire and is sinking. The only way out is through the porthole."
Lee pointed to the truck tire that was suspended between two vertical logs. "Your mission is to get your squad through the porthole and
to the life boat on the other side. You will wear your helmet, but no
other gear.

"Coordinating instructions: One, do not touch the wire cables that
support the tire. Two, do not touch the tire tread. Imagine that the
tire's hole is a porthole in the bulkhead of a ship. Three, all recruits
must go feet first through the tire. Four, do not throw recruits
through the tire. Good to go?"

"Yes, Sergeant," answered Nushi. He was another good recruit.
He couldn't perform close-order drill to save his life, but he was in
good shape and needed little supervision when given a task. He
joined, like most did, out of high school. He said that he joined only
for the education benefits, but he could have received the same financial aid from any of the other services without some of the demands that came with being a Marine. Like most, he joined because
he wanted to be something special, but was still concerned about
failing. His family had immigrated from the former Yugoslavia before he was born. A proud family, two of his brothers had become
Marines too. His father owned a contracting business, and Nushi
was often placed in charge of work sites, supervising his father's
workers. This developed in him a natural ability to lead, as well as
an impressive work ethic. He knew how to motivate others by the

simple use of a compliment and setting an example by participating in the dirty work.

"BEFORE YOU TAKE ANY ACTION, YOU MUST BRIEF ME ON YOUR PLAN," said Sergeant Lee.

Nushi had little difficulty communicating his plan to the other recruits. The recruits would simply lift each other up and through the tire. The first one or two would need to complete it with little help on the other side, but most would need help to get them through. The hardest part, as with the last obstacle, would be getting the last few men through the tire. Nushi told the others that he wanted two of the smaller recruits to go last, but he would be the very last one. There was some debate whether a larger and stronger recruit should be last. Nushi was insistent, however. He felt that a smaller recruit would be easier to get through than a large one.

After Nushi told Sergeant Lee his plan, the group began to move through the obstacle. He sent two strong recruits first. Not only would they be able to help the weaker ones when they came through, they were also heavier and needed more recruits to lift them to "porthole" height. The way the tire was positioned and the feet-first passage, made it necessary that the men be lifted into the tire. It was impossible to do it alone without breaking the rules by touching the wire or the tire tread. When there was only Nushi and another remaining on the "sinking" side of the obstacle, it was obvious why he wanted the smaller recruits to go last. It was easy for Nushi to pick the man up and hand him through to the others. Now he was the last and the others chuckled as he explained how he intended to get himself through. As silly as it sounded, it made enough sense to work. He faced the tire and leaned forward into a handstand position. Holding the handstand for a second, he allowed himself to fall so the backs of his legs hit the tire. The recruits, some standing on the backs of others, grabbed his legs and positioned them so the feet hung out the other side of the tire and his calves rested inside it. Then Nushi just did a sit-up as the other recruits pulled him through. It was a little painful on his butt, but he was soon on the other side with his squad.

"Well, that was pretty interesting," laughed Sergeant Lee. "Sit down by the gear and take your helmets off for the debrief." The recruits were obviously proud of themselves. They had made it through this one with no trouble, but it was still early and there were forty-nine hours remaining in the Crucible. "What kind of difficulties would you have encountered if you did not have your team to support you?"

"A few of us might have been able to do it without help, but most would have died when the ship sank," said one recruit.

"We had to use teamwork."

"You needed to work together, but don't forget that individual skills can help the team. Especially Nushi's acrobatic act, sort of like Corporal Mackie and his shooting," said Sergeant Lee. "Think about what was going through his mind when he was performing his duties. Even when the deck of the ship was being raked by shellfire, he still held his position and continued to fire. Then later on in the fight, the ship received a hit that caused a secondary explosion and many casualties. The ship was severely damaged and many of the leaders were dead, so Mackie rallied the survivors, carried off the dead and wounded, and got three of the USS *Galena*'s guns back in action. What else is special about Corporal Mackie?"

"He was the first United States Marine ever to be awarded the Medal of Honor," answered Simms.

"That's right, where did we learn that?"

"From the Marine Corps history classes in the first phase of training, Sergeant."

"Now put yourself in Corporal Mackie's shoes and imagine what it would be like."

"It would be difficult to keep panic from setting in," said Nushi.

"Like you said, some individuals could get themselves out in time, but if the squad doesn't work together many will die. But Mackie did even more than that, didn't he?" asked Sergeant Lee.

"He could have protected himself when the deck of the ship was being raked with fire, but he continued firing at the enemy instead," said Simms.

"He even took charge when a leader was needed," said Nushi.

"Just like you did, right?" Sergeant Lee said to Nushi. "Nothing new though, right?"

"Not to Marines," said a recruit.

"You don't even need to start talking about a war to find instances of Marines acting like this. One of the units in my regiment had a helicopter full of Marines go down during a routine flight off the coast of Africa in 1992. An explosion engulfed the aircraft in flames, instantly killing three Marines onboard. They lost power and crashed violently into shark-infested waters. The cabin flooded instantaneously, the weight of the engines flipped the helicopter upside down, and they began to sink in the water. Think about what that would be like; flying to burning to crashing to sinking. All of it happen in a matter of seconds, too." Sergeant Lee paused to let the recruits make a comment or ask a question.

"Did anyone live, Sergeant?" asked Simms.

"Actually, most of them did, and you know why?"

"Because they worked together," said one of the recruits.

"These Devil Dogs were *not* going to let their buddies die. Even though most of them were severely burned and their life jackets were shredded, they still had the presence of mind to help each other. Of the eighteen on board, fourteen survived. There was even a point where two of the Marines went back into the sinking aircraft to pull out a badly burned Marine trapped in the wreckage. Why did they do that?"

"Marines take care of their own, Sergeant!" said Nushi.

"Darn right we do," said Sergeant Lee, "and there are other ways we do that beyond courage in a stressful situation. What about Corporal Mackie's marksmanship skills, how did he use them to take care of others?"

"He kept up the fire at the enemy," said a recruit.

"His skill could be counted on," said Sergeant Lee. "What's that called?"

"Competence, Sergeant," said one man.

"That's part of commitment," said another.

Commitment is the spirit of determination and dedication within members of a force of arms that leads to professionalism and mastery of the art of war. It leads to the highest order of discipline for unit and self and is the ingredient that enables twenty-four-hour-a-day dedication to Corps and country. It is an unrelenting determination to achieve a standard of excellence in every endeavor through personal pride and concern for others. Commitment is the value that establishes the Marine as the warrior and citizen that others strive to emulate.

"Right," said Sergeant Lee. "Having the dedication to maintain and improve to a level that is second to none. That should be your own goal with the rifle by building off the marksmanship skills you developed when we were on the rifle range."

Marksmanship training is broken into three parts that are designed to teach recruits the basic fundamentals of marksmanship. It takes place in the second phase of training at Camp Pendleton. The first part, "grass week," is one week and consists of classes on firing positions, safety procedures, marksmanship skills, and range regulations. In the second week, "firing week," the recruits practice firing on the known-distance range and qualify with the M16A2 service rifle. The third week, "field firing," teaches rifle presentation and engagement techniques in a combat environment.

For a recruit to graduate he must qualify on the known-distance range. Each fires fifty rounds at a value of five points apiece, so a maximum score is 250 points. Very few recruits ever get close to that, with most firing a 200 or better. They fire from the two-, three-, and five-hundred yard lines at targets smaller in size than the average man. A score of 190 is needed to qualify as a marksman, 210 for sharpshooter, 220 for expert.

Those having serious problems receive remedial training from a primary marksmanship instructor (PMI). A most effective tool is an indoor marksmanship training system, a computerized big screen that allows the PMI to closely analyze the recruit's habits. It is uncommon that a PMI doesn't get a recruit qualified. Occasionally a man is unable to qualify and is discharged from the Marine Corps. There are no waivers granted for those who cannot shoot.

"Any more questions or comments?" asked Sergeant Lee. It was almost 0700 and the recruits were ready to go. They didn't want to talk anymore; they were ready for the next challenge.

The walk to the next warrior station would be a quick one, but Sergeant Lee noticed that one of the recruits was limping soon after they stepped off. Upon questioning he learned that the young man was in severe pain. He had twisted his ankle during the early morning movement to the bivouac site, but was trying to continue.

Sergeant Lee called for a Navy corpsman[2] who quickly determined that the recruit was seriously hurt. The ankle might be broken, but even if sprained there was little hope for the man to return to the Crucible. He was sent to the medical clinic and then to the medical rehabilitation platoon back at MCRD, San Diego. After a few weeks he might be ready to begin the Crucible again.

2. Medical and religious personnel are provided to the Marine Corps by the U.S. Navy. Chaplains and corpsmen and women serve with all Marine units, accompanying them into combat for spiritual and physical care. They are an essential part of the Corps' effectiveness.

4

Sergeant Gonzalez's Crossing

By early 1967, more than 67,000 Marines were in Vietnam and the M16 service rifle began replacing the sturdy M14. Ten Marines had already earned the Medal of Honor, but there were still another fifteen who would receive the award before the year ended. I Corps was referred to as "Marineland," and in the spring an isolated firebase at Khe Sanh began to come under continuous attack.

By 1968, Marine casualties exceeded those suffered in Korea, and Khe Sanh was under a full siege. The base was in jeopardy, leading some to a comparison with the French defeat at Dien Bien Phu. The Tet truce offered the possibility of some break in the fighting, but it would prove to be an unfulfilled hope. The enemy would use the cover of the truce to infiltrate soldiers south to the villages and hamlets within striking distance of major cities. The attack began on 29 January with rocket attacks against major installations and soon consumed most of South Vietnam.

Early on 30 January, more than 60,000 enemy attacked every important American base and most provincial and district capitals throughout South Vietnam. Many South Vietnamese troops who were supposed to be defending the cities were absent for the Tet holiday. Rockets and mortars hammered Marine aviation units at Da Nang, Marble Mountain, and Chu Lai as the communists tried to reduce America's ability to influence the battle with its air superiority.

A team of Vietcong commandos blasted their way into the American embassy in Saigon, killing several Army soldiers and wounding one of the three Marines on duty. The invaders held the embassy compound for more than six hours, shocking Americans back home who watched the drama on television.

44

Enemy forces were stopped short of seizing Da Nang and Saigon, but were successful in taking the ancient capital of Hue. Enemy infiltrators were able to sneak into the city in civilian clothing, only to change into uniforms and immediately grasp control over the majority of the city. Marine forces were ordered to liberate the city, and they began fighting through scattered resistance toward Hue.

It took more than a month of fighting to recapture Hue, with bitter fighting in the city reminiscent of experiences from the Korean War. It was house-to-house and street-to-street, with the odds against the attackers. At times, Marines had to use helicopters and landing craft to launch new attacks. On 2 March the battle was finally over. The Marines had 142 killed and 857 wounded, and the ancient city was in ruins. A Marine casualty being evacuated from Hue was asked by reporters how many times he'd been wounded, only to respond, *"you mean today?"*

"This obstacle is named in honor of Alfredo Gonzalez of Edinburg, Texas," said Sergeant Lee. It was 0700, the recruits already had hiked more than six miles and missed their first meal. "He was born 23 May 1946 and joined the Marine Corps in June 1965. He arrived in Vietnam in July of 1967 for service with 1st Battalion, 1st Marines.

The President of the United States in the name of The Congress takes pleasure in presenting the Medal of Honor posthumously to Sergeant Alfredo Gonzalez, United States Marine Corps, for service set forth in the following citation:

For conspicuous gallantry and intrepidity at the risk of his life above and beyond the call of duty while serving as platoon commander, 3d Platoon, Company A, 1st Battalion, 1st Marines, 1st Marine Division (Rein), FMF [Fleet Marine Force], in the Republic of Vietnam. On 31 January 1968, during the initial phase of Operation Hue City, Sergeant Gonzalez's unit was formed as a reaction force and deployed to Hue to relieve the pressure on the beleaguered city. While moving by truck convoy along Route No. 1, near the village of Lang Van Lrong, the Marines received a heavy volume of enemy fire. Sergeant Gonzalez aggressively maneuvered the Marines in his platoon, and directed their fire until the area was cleared of snipers. Immediately after crossing a river south of Hue, the column was again hit by intense enemy fire. One of the Marines on top of a tank was wounded and fell to the ground in an exposed position. With complete disregard for his own safety, Sergeant Gonzalez ran through the fire-swept area to the assistance of his injured comrade. He lifted him up, and though receiving fragmentation wounds during the rescue, he carried the wounded Marine to a covered position for treatment. Due to the increased volume and accuracy of enemy fire from a fortified machine-gun bunker on the side of the road, the company was temporarily halted. Realizing the gravity of the situation, Sergeant Gonzalez exposed himself to the enemy fire and moved his platoon along the east side of a bordering rice paddy to a dike directly across from the bunker. Though fully aware of the danger involved, he moved to the fire-swept road and destroyed the hostile position with hand grenades. Although seriously wounded again on 3 February, he steadfastly refused medical treatment and continued to supervise his men and lead the attack. On 4 February, the enemy had again pinned the company down, inflicting heavy casualties with automatic weapons and rocket fire. Sergeant Gonzalez, utilizing a number of light antitank assault weapons, fearlessly moved from position to position firing numerous rounds at the heavily fortified enemy emplacements. He successfully knocked out a rocket position and suppressed much of the enemy force before falling mortally wounded. The heroism, courage, and dynamic leadership displayed by Sergeant Gonzalez reflected great credit upon himself and the Marine Corps and were in keeping with the highest traditions of the United States Naval Service. He gallantly gave his life for his country.

Signed, Richard M. Nixon[1]

Simms counted the number of wounds in his head—*three!* Sergeant Gonzalez was wounded no less than three separate times

1. Medal of Honor citation from *The Congressional Medal of Honor, The Names, The Deeds* (Chico, Calif., Sharp and Dunnigan, 1988) 66.

within a four-day period. Refusing medical attention and evacuation the entire time, he not only continued fighting, but also remained in command of an entire platoon. Even more impressive, he had only two and a half years in the Corps, was only twenty-one years old, and he was performing duties intended for a commissioned officer.

"Smith, you're going to be the leader for this next problem," said Sergeant Lee. The obstacle in front of the squad consisted of three small tables arranged in a triangle formation and separated from each other by a distance of ten to fifteen feet. A rope, suspended from logs overhead, was positioned in the middle of the three tables.

Smith was the type who blended into the crowd, one of three recruits who caused the drill instructors to be confused, as they kept forgetting their names. Each platoon seemed to have a few who never actually stood out. He was an average recruit, who most likely would be a pretty good Marine. One reason he was so easy to forget was that he always did what he was supposed to without additional instruction or close supervision. If he had been a little better, he would have been a squad leader candidate.

"Your squad has been moving through a chemically contaminated area on the way to assist another squad pinned down by enemy forces near platform three," Sergeant Lee pointed to one of the three small tables. "A decontamination station is at platform two," he pointed to another table, "but you're over there on platform one" he pointed to the last table. "Your mission is to decontaminate your team along with your equipment and then assist the squad that is pinned down. You will wear your helmet, load-bearing vest, and an M40 gas mask.

"Coordinating instructions: One, team members will wear a gas mask from platform one to platform two. Two, you may remove your mask after reaching platform two. Three, if a team member or his gear touches the ground, that person or piece of gear is eliminated from the problem. Four, you may retrieve the rope to start. Do you have any questions?"

"No, Sergeant," said Smith. He was uncertain about what exactly was expected of him, and he also couldn't really think of a question to ask. He was not a "people person," but he knew how to think. A bright student, Smith was headed to college, planning to use money earned in the Marine Corps Reserve to help pay for tuition. He worked out the details before he even spoke to the recruiter, researching military pay scales on the Internet. He knew that the other services were capable of providing the same benefits as the Marines, but he always dreamed of one day being a Marine.

Sergeant Gonzalez's citation reminded Smith of a Marine who received the Bronze Star for valor in the African city of Monrovia. When Smith was in high school he began to read the newspaper and watch the evening news regularly. Marines evacuating civilians from the war-torn country of Liberia was at the forefront of the news in mid-1996, and Smith found himself fascinated by the Marines' operations reported by the media.

On 30 April 1996, Marine corporal Jason Farrand was manning an observation post from one of the many rooms of the U.S. embassy in Liberia. Fighting between rival Liberian factions had become common in the immediate area of the embassy, making things dangerous for those inside. Farrand was looking through a scope when he was suddenly shot in the neck. The force broke the legs of the chair he was sitting in, knocking him to the ground. Other Marines came to his aid and evacuated him to the aid station for medical attention.

Farrand was lucky. The bullet had entered his collar bone and exited through his neck, two millimeters in any other direction he would likely have bled to death within minutes. Navy corpsmen were able to stabilize him and give life-saving first aid, but Farrand needed more medical attention. Fearing that he was about to be evacuated back to the ship, and concerned that his brother Marines were in danger, Corporal Farrand grabbed his gear and ran from the aid station. He made it back to his unit just when two rival factions numbering at least 100 fighters grew dangerously close. The Marines held their fire as the two factions fought on the streets outside the embassy. Finally, one group overran the other, but then made a tragic error and began to fire on the Marines. Farrand fired back and the other seven Marines joined in immediately, driving the Liberians back.

"You paying attention to me, Smith?" barked Sergeant Lee.

"Yes, sir," Smith said, locking his body at the position of attention.

"*Hello,* correct yourself," said Sergeant Lee.

"Yes, Sergeant," replied Smith, relaxing his body so he was no longer at attention. He realized that he needed to stop thinking like a recruit and start thinking like a Marine.

"Before you take any action, you must brief me on your plan." Sergeant Lee looked at his watch. "You have two minutes."

Sergeant Lee stepped out of the way, leaving Smith alone to adjust to the burden of command. The recruits talked among themselves, discussing options for the plan. They usually worked well together, and leaders were willing to listen to the input from the group. They soon had a plan and Smith told Sergeant Lee how they were going to accomplish their mission.

The recruits put on their gas masks and collected around table number one. Only three recruits could fit on the table at one time, so the others formed in a line to wait their turn. Smith took the rope first and swung toward the second table, only to just miss it. The rope was positioned to make it look easy, but it actually swung at an awkward angle. As he swung back toward the first table, one of the other recruits grabbed his foot and pulled him back in to safety.

"Let me try it," said another man, his voice difficult to understand through the gas mask. He took Smith's place on the rope and swung off in the direction of table number two. He came a little closer than did Smith, touching it with his foot, but was unable to make it. Simms and the others failed to catch him when the rope swung back toward table number one, leaving him hanging on the rope in the middle of the sawdust pit.

"You're out," said Sergeant Lee when the man's foot touched the ground. One of the team members was "dead," and they all were still on the first table.

Smith grabbed the rope to try again, swinging out at a different angle, but was still unsuccessful. "Give me a push," he said to the other recruits. His third attempt was successful. They were learning the importance of teamwork.

"Now, that table is the decontamination site, so you can take off your gas mask," said Sergeant Lee. "But you can only grab a contaminated person if you have your mask on."

"You need to give each other a push," said Simms to the others. Now with Smith on the second table, it was easier to get the others across. Recruits from table one would push the recruit on the rope, while Smith grabbed them and helped them onto table two. After there were a few on table two, Smith directed Simms to head for table three. It was an easier swing than from table one to two and he made it on the first attempt.

The squad was making its way through the obstacle pretty easily when adversity hit them. A recruit on the second table tried to grab the one on the rope, only to be pulled off the table. Both touched the ground and were eliminated from the problem. Three were now "dead."

"Someone needs to hold onto whomever is grabbing," said one of the last two recruits on the first table.

"What?" said Smith, unable to clearly understand the recruit through his gas mask. The recruit on table one tried to say it again, but he still didn't clearly state his message.

"Hold on to the grabber," the recruit on table one said clearly after lifting his gas mask to be heard.

"You're out," said Sergeant Lee. "You're still in a chemically contaminated area, so taking your mask off just removed you from the problem." He paid the price of not thinking about the consequences of an action.

Now there was only one man left on the first table, and, unfortunately, he was one of the weaker recruits. He tried to swing toward the second table, but failed to get close because there was no one to give him a push. As he swung back toward table one he came near enough to table three for one of the recruits to grab him.

"You're out, too," said Sergeant Lee to the recruit who grabbed the one on the rope. "He's still contaminated and hasn't been through the decontamination site, so now you're contaminated, right?"

"Yes, sir," said the latest loss to the team. Again, failure of an individual to think clearly and quickly cost the team a resource.

The recruit on the rope was sent back to table one to try again. After several hopeless attempts the recruit lost his grip and fell to the ground. Six members of the team were now lost. The remaining recruits finished their movement from table two to table three. Sergeant Lee had the recruits put away the gas masks, then sit down in a semicircle for the debrief.

"Was the obstacle easy or difficult?" asked Sergeant Lee.

"It was easy once I figured out how the rope swings at a weird angle," said Smith.

"Was it harder than it looks?"

"It was a lot harder than it looks," said Smith.

"Imagine how hard it seemed for Sergeant Gonzalez to move across that fire-swept area to help that wounded Marine. In combat the easy often seems difficult and the difficult can seem impossible. What else did he have working against him?"

Smith thought about how difficult it would have been for Corporal Farrand to ignore a near deadly wound to *run* back and join the fight in Liberia. He made a comment about it and Sergeant Lee told him to tell the squad the story.

"They were both wounded when they did these things," said a recruit.

"That's right, but they overcame that to take care of brother Marines," said Sergeant Lee. "If you don't remember from Gonzalez's citation, he was actually wounded on that first day and again four days later, but he still kept fighting until he was killed the next day. Was Sergeant Gonzalez committed to the team?" The recruits all agreed. "What did you do for each other that was important for success? Was just knowing the right way to swing on the rope enough?"

"We also needed to give each other a push, Sergeant."

"So we needed teamwork, right?" said Sergeant Lee. "How did you think that you did as the leader, Smith?"

"I was able to do it with just a little bit of help," answered Smith.

"Right, but how did you do at leading? You demonstrated some good courage by having the initiative to be the first to try. Sergeant Gonzalez was leading from the front, too, when he attacked the enemy rocket positions. What I want to know is how you led?" Lee had to be careful to make his point without humiliating Smith. This would only make the recruits reluctant to make decisions or use initiative, because they would be concerned about being embarrassed during the debrief. Mistakes were important because they provided learning opportunities that would make the team stronger.

"Okay, I guess," said Smith. "We were able to get to the other side of the obstacle so we could help the other squad that was pinned down by the enemy."

"But we lost six, didn't we?"

"Yes, Sergeant."

"Why did we lose the first one?" asked Sergeant Lee.

"Because we weren't paying attention, and we didn't catch him," said a recruit.

"That's right," said Sergeant Lee. "The team let him down, right?"

"Yes, but I should have made sure that someone was looking out for him because I was the leader," said Smith.

"It's all of our faults," said Nushi. "We should have been looking out for each other regardless of who was the leader."

"So we could have been more committed to the team," said Sergeant Lee. "That much is pretty obvious now, but what are you," he pointed to the recruits, "demonstrating now?" They sat in silence and waited for him to clarify his question. They didn't see where he was going with the discussion. "What are you demonstrating now, during this debrief, Simms? What core value?"

"Uhhmmm . . . courage?" said Simms.

"Sort of, but what I'm looking for is for some of you to personally accept the consequences for your decisions and actions."

"Honor," said Smith.

Honor is the bedrock of a Marine's character, the quality that guides Marines to exemplify the ultimate in ethical and moral behavior. It means to never lie, cheat, or steal, and to abide by an uncompromising code of integrity; to always respect human dignity and have concern for others. The qualities of maturity, dedication, trust, and dependability commit Marines to act responsibly and be accountable for their actions. Also, they must be able to fulfill obligations and hold others accountable for their actions.

"In fact, several of you are showing honor, because you're demonstrating responsibility by being accountable for your actions." Sergeant Lee nodded his head, "Yep, you all are actually arguing over whose fault it is. Not the way you may have a few months ago. No one is saying 'it's your fault' and pointing fingers, is he? We're actually arguing by saying, 'no, it's my fault.'"

Personal accountability is difficult to instill in today's youth. With the lawsuits from accidents originating from a stupid act of the plaintiff, it was not surprising to see how a young man would find it strange to admit when he was wrong. The immediate response in an auto accident is to make the other seem to be at fault. Many daytime television shows create a "victim" mentality in viewers, again making it acceptable to blame something, anything, other than one's own conduct.

"What about when we lost the next two? Why did that happen?"

"Because we weren't being smart," said the man who was pulled from the table. "We should have seen that someone could get pulled off the table like that."

"We should have been looking out for each other at all times," said Sergeant Lee, "and as the leader you need to be thinking about the team and how to best employ your strengths to overcome your weaknesses. Sergeant Gonzalez did that when he aggressively maneuvered his platoon to clear the enemy during that first part of the citation. He's up front and leading by example, but he's using his men where they will best serve the team. How could you have used the individuals of the team in a better way?"

"I shouldn't have gone last," said the last recruit who 'died' during the obstacle.

"Well, I shouldn't have taken off my mask," said the man who was trying to talk to the others trying to grab the recruit on the rope.

"I shouldn't have tried to grab a contaminated private either," said another.

"This is a thinking man's game, isn't it?"

"Yes, because if we aren't thinking, then we end up hurting the squad," said Simms.

"Well, not just the squad, but who else?" asked Lee. Nobody answered. "What about that squad we're coming to help? Are they better off if six of us show up, or if twelve of us do?"

"Definitely twelve," said Smith.

"Screwing up like we did hurts our team, but it also hurts other Marines who are depending on us," said Simms.

"To do things better in the future we need to evaluate what the strengths and weaknesses of the individuals are. Some of you might be good at something like this obstacle, but bad somewhere else. If one of us is apt to have problems, then we need to identify them and put them in a position where the team can get them through the obstacle. So in this problem, if we were to do it again, what would you do differently?"

"I would pick out who was to go first and who to be last," said Smith. "Those who might have problems should go somewhere in the middle."

"How do you pick the men who go in the middle?" asked Sergeant Lee.

"We could ask each other who could have a problem," said a recruit.

"And admitting that we might need some help doing something means we'll be pointing out a personal weakness. That takes moral courage, doesn't it? It's not easy to say 'hey, I might need some help on this one,' but it's part of teamwork."

These points may seem minor, but they were tangible experiences to which the recruits could relate. They had plenty of classes about being a Marine, about having honor, courage, and commitment, but now they could compare what they learned with what they were doing. Hindsight being twenty-twenty, it was easy for the recruits to look back and see the mistakes they had made. Talking was easy, but acting was an entirely different experience. If they were really learning, it would show in their performance on future obstacles.

"Are there any questions before we move on to the next obstacle?" asked Sergeant Lee.

"What was it like when the Marine was hurt in the minefield in Kuwait?" asked Simms. "Was it difficult to find the courage to go help him?"

Sergeant Lee was surprised by the question. He didn't know that the senior drill instructor told the platoon about his heroic act. Embarrassed to discuss it, he said the first thing that came to his mind, "I was more afraid of letting everyone else know I was scared." He smiled and paused for a second. "It's difficult to explain, but when you're in a situation like that, it's hard *not* to do something. I once heard a Medal of Honor recipient tell a group of people that he would have run away if no one else had been watching. He was kidding, of course, but I think I know what he meant. I was probably more terrified about my Marines knowing I was shaking than I was of being blown up.

"No more questions after that one. Saddle up, we're moving in two minutes."

5

Endurance Course

There really isn't an official endurance course in the Crucible itself, but there is a portion that is so difficult that the officers and drill instructors started referring to it as such. The members of 4th squad would be physically challenged with the next three Crucible stations, much more than they'd experienced during the warrior stations.

The first station is the bayonet assault course, a series of exercises to test the skills needed to fight effectively in close combat. In teams of four men, the recruits fix bayonets and attack through an obstacle course of barbed wire, culverts, and logs. Their physical endurance is tested by crawling under the wire and through the culverts, only to meet logs that need to be scaled. Throughout the entire course there are dummies, "enemy soldiers," that the trainees have to muster the strength to attack with bayonets. Just as they climb from under or over an obstacle, near exhausted and ready to take a break and catch their breath, they instead charge forward to attack the next enemy position.

Immediately after the bayonet-assault course, the squad puts their field packs on their backs and makes the one-and-a-half-mile hike to the infiltration course. Another collection of barbed-wire obstacles and culverts, it is intended to replicate the obstacles Marines meet when attacking a fortified position. Beyond the physical challenges of the wire, logs, and culverts, in true Marine Corps style, there is the mental challenge of a sprinkler system. It was installed to ensure the recruits always have a fresh layer of mud and water to make the experience even more miserable. They not only negotiate the course, but also drag heavy ammunition cans (20 pounds) and crates (30 to 40 pounds) with them. Halfway through, one of the recruits becomes a "casualty," requiring the others to drag him to the finish. Pneumatic machine guns fire over their heads and demolition charges explode all around them to represent incoming high-explosive rounds. The sight, sounds, and smells are enough to terrify a person, but the recruits band together to get through the course as a team.

Again with no rest, they pick up their packs and move to the next and possibly most challenging course. This consists of more barbed wire and obstacles coupled with water and mud to form a challenge that stretches for hundreds of meters through one of the many draws at Camp Pendleton. They arrive at the day movement course near exhaustion, covered in mud and sweat, and on this course the pressure is turned up further. One of the team becomes a "casualty" immediately and the others are to carry him to an evacuation helicopter to save his life. From the start point the recruits can see the hulk of an old Marine Corps helicopter, seemingly far too distant to reach in the twenty-five-minute time limit. To make it even more difficult, there are again a variety of heavy ammunition cans and crates for the men to bring with them. They fight to drag their "wounded" comrade under the wire, over the walls, through the water—always conscious of the fact that time is not on their side. One walks into a trip wire and triggers a small explosion to simulate a booby trap. Now two are casualties, increasing the demand on the squad. If they work together and sacrifice, they will make it in time. If they fail to be a team and instead think as individuals, the helicopter will leave without their "wounded" buddies.

These three courses often serve as a turning point for the Crucible. For the members of 4th squad, it signaled the end of a certain sense of adventure and made them realize that the Crucible was intended to be a challenging course, a challenge so large that it held the potential to break them physically, mentally, and spiritually. This was one reason why the drill instructors were so hard on them during the past eleven-plus weeks of training.

Although the Crucible is the final test, it is also the established goal, and drill instructors focus their attention and training on building recruits capable of living up to the challenge. It is designed to be so demanding that it resembles the demands of combat, without actually placing the recruits' lives in jeopardy. Marines have always finished their intensive training with some kind of final exercise. The Crucible is today's final test for a new Marine.

It was now 1000, eight hours since reveille and the men were only beginning. The Crucible wasn't even close to a quarter of the way done and the recruits were already hungry, wet, and tired. They'd hiked about ten miles, and the blisters were beginning to form on the feet that they thought were tough and ready to handle any challenge. For some, every step brought pain. Others saw the pain and wondered how much longer it would be until their feet started to break and blister, putting them also in pain.

The Medal of Honor citations from the warrior stations would continue to be used, reminding the recruits that their pain and suffering paled in comparison to that which Marines from the past had endured. They were only the tip of the proverbial iceberg, however. Only eleven Medal of Honor citations were used during the Crucible, but 294 Marines have received the award since Corporal Mackie received his in 1863. Two Marines[1] have been awarded the Medal twice: Dan Daily received his first in China, 1900, and the second during the Haitian Campaign in 1915; Smedley Butler earned one in Vera Cruz in 1914, and the second during the Haitian Campaign in 1915.

Almost instinctively, the recruits began to grab a quick bite from their MREs when they were finally done with the third event, only to have Sergeant Lee stop them. There was very little time before they were to move again and their weapons needed to be cleaned. Their hunger would linger as they tried to ensure that their weapons could be employed. This was a lesson that would be remembered if the future Marines ever found themselves in combat hungry and tired but with a dirty weapon—*the weapon always comes first.*

The increased hardship caused stress that was different from that created previously by the drill instructors, but stress that could be handled much the same way. These recruits were expected to use

---

1. Five Marines technically received two Medals of Honor when the Army and the Navy had separate awards, but that was for the same heroic act.

all the skills they had learned to overcome the new challenges. As they became more tired, they became more stressed, causing panic and rage to increase. Luckily, the drill instructors had trained them to overcome adversity and operate in a chaotic and hostile environment, and to always control their emotions. Self-control was an important skill.

A Marine standing guard over a food distribution operation during a humanitarian mission doesn't have the luxury of having feelings. If a teenage boy came up and threw a rock at him, hitting him in the face, maybe drawing blood, the Marine's reaction would have to be controlled. The whole incident could be in plain view of hundreds of people, and captured on live international television. If he lost his temper while holding a loaded assault weapon, the child might be killed or seriously injured. This would be a tragedy for the child and his family, but a catastrophe for American foreign policy. Becoming emotional would only increase the likelihood of future incidents, because deciding to attack a foe who is perceived to be weak is easy to do.

Recruit-training squad bays in the first week of training have numerous incidents of recruits crying, having tantrums, or even violently lashing out at their drill instructors. The drill instructors' responses, much like the Marine at a food distribution point, have to be a controlled and disciplined example. Nothing confuses a young man more than to have a drill instructor laugh at him when the recruit tries to manipulate the situation with emotion or anger. For the recruit, it had frequently been a source of power with parents and teachers, but not with a drill instructor who says something in response like, "I've faced off against Iraqi tanks, do you think the F-word is going to hurt me? *Ha ha!*" The recruit learns to expect to be worked harder and that such behavior only makes things worse.

Recruits are also surprised by how little their drill instructors curse or swear. Surely, there is the occasional slip, but they become aware of the absence of swearing overall. As with everything else, a reason lies behind the no-swearing policy. The standard operating procedure from as far back as the 1940s forbade the use of vulgar language, but many would debate how often the rule was followed. One certainly could argue that there was a time when the eloquent use of ·

colorful words contributed to the culture shock that recruits experienced. Those days are long past. That was a time when such language was rare in American society, but unfortunately, that is not the case today. The F-word is used like a comma in teenage speech, thrown out every few words, and characters in prime-time television shows and movies use language that would have caused a parent to slap a child twenty years ago. Today, drill instructors swearing and cursing would reinforce a recruit's bad habits and make him comfortable with his new world, reducing the culture shock. Disciplining a recruit for swearing has the opposite effect, one more tool to throw a recruit off balance, especially when the swearing results in the recruit receiving incentive training, punishment through physical exercise commonly known as "IT."

Simms experienced this scenario himself. Calling his mother a "bitch" or swearing at her would make her lock herself in her room and cry, leaving him to do whatever he wanted. He learned the hard way that he lost control of the situation by acting that way with the drill instructors. When Simms was overheard saying "bullshit" about the guide's instructions to the platoon, the drill instructor laughed and walked away. Simms felt like a little boy and would have preferred to have the sergeant yell at him. About an hour later, when he thought the drill instructor had forgotten his childish behavior, he was called to the quarter deck of the squad bay to "*BEGIN!*" Begin with physical exercises—jumping jacks, push-ups, flutter kicks, and running in place.

Incentive training is awarded to a recruit for several reasons: sometimes, a response to a specific act; other times for no apparent reason. Unexpected adversity that seems to have no logic comes in much the same way that a piece of shrapnel simply picks out one victim from a group, or the way a sniper shoots at someone just because he's there. Working through unexpected adversity is what really distinguishes Marines from the average human. Anyone can prepare for hardships he knows are coming, but it takes someone special to thrive through unexpected and seemingly unfair treatment.

Incentive training is most effective when it is immediate in response to a specific act. On one occasion Simms saluted Lieutenant Harris while in the field, after being told several times not to do so.

Such conduct is dangerous in a combat zone, because it signals out officers, making them easy targets for the enemy. Before the lieutenant could correct him, Simms heard his drill instructor yelling a full 300 meters away. *"EMPTY YOUR POCKETS INTO YOUR HELMET, SIMMS.*[2] *EMPTY YOUR POCKETS AND BEGIN! BEEGINNN!"* screamed his drill instructor as he narrowed the 300 meters at a full sprint. By the time he was 200 meters away the contents of his pockets were in his helmet and he was doing jumping jacks. At 100 meters Simms was on his fifth and a few seconds later the drill instructor was in his face.

"THIS IS WHAT IT TAKES, RIGHT, SIMMS?" Sweat pouring off his face, spitting with every word and still catching his breath after the sprint. Simms painfully struggled through the various torturous exercises. *"THIS IS WHAT IT TAKES. WE TELL YOU AND TELL YOU, BUT IT TAKES PAIN FOR YOU TO LEARN, DOESN'T IT? DOESN'T IT! I SHOULD ONLY NEED TO TELL YOU ONCE. FAILURE TO FOLLOW SIMPLE INSTRUCTIONS, SIMMS. FAILURE TO FOLLOW SIMPLE INSTRUCTIONS. YOU'RE WASTING MY TIME AND PREVENTING ME FROM TEACHING YOU OTHER THINGS!"* Simms didn't salute another officer in the field and never would again.

These experiences are what really make Marine Corps recruit training; no single event causes it to be what it is. Taking almost 40,000 young men and women each year and training them to a level of excellence that makes them actually believe that they can do anything as challenging as the Crucible sounds impossible. Street punks, jocks, honor students, and couch potatoes all need to be shaped, developed, and trained in eleven short weeks. They must be prepared to step into the wild and live off the material they carry on their backs, while suffering great hardships for absolutely no reason. Three months earlier many of these recruits probably would have already quit the Crucible. They would have broken down, lashed out,

---

2. A safety requirement of the depot's standard operating procedure so recruits didn't accidentally stab themselves with an ink pen or some other object.

and failed miserably. They would not have been willing to take up the challenge to become Marines.

The transformation that occurs in eleven weeks is nothing short of a miracle, all due to the example set by the drill instructors. A Marine Corps drill instructor is a professional who has no equal. He is fully committed to doing everything within his or her power to make a young American into a Marine. Often they can be seen spending extra time training and teaching those not up to par with the others. Sometimes the help comes in the form of a fatherly talk, while at other times it is with an IT session. Regardless, the fact that the drill instructor accepts no excuses and continues to try is what is really important. Recruits make up excuses for their failures: *I've always been a slow learner, I'm not athletically inclined* . . . The excuses usually meet with a drill instructor who points out that the man needs to try harder. When a weakness is identified, there is no reason for not overcoming it. The recruits see how this attitude causes themselves or others to rise to new heights of performance. This proves that anything can be achieved if the men put their minds to it and practice teamwork.

There are some who are untrainable, however, those who must be discharged. There is a point where it becomes apparent that it is no longer fair to the recruit or the Marine Corps that an individual continue training. Usually it is a recruit who is so undisciplined that he continues to respond with insubordination and disrespect. Others cannot handle the stress, requiring a visit to the depot's mental health unit for an evaluation to determine if they are fit for military service. Platoon 3075 had a few recruits who fit into these categories.

Recruit Boon did everything from rolling his eyes at the drill instructors to throwing a canteen at a wall. His conduct was disruptive to the platoon, but the staff continued to leave him with the platoon for several days after his first violent outburst. The drill instructors did not want the recruits to think that they would be able to get out of boot camp with such conduct. They also wanted to make it clear that they had given Boon every opportunity to be a Marine. Finally, after another explosion of violence, military police were called and Boon was taken away.

Boon's fate would be decided in the first few hours. He either would be discharged quickly, or he would go to a court-martial and spend some time in the brig before going home. Punishing Boon wasn't the deciding factor; what was best for the Corps was.

Recruit Kenny was so stressed by the drill instructors that he was unable to function properly. He locked up and was not able to speak, even when the lieutenant tried to sit him down to relax him. His problem was so severe that he needed to visit a Navy psychologist before the drill instructors continued to try to train him. The doctor spent less than an hour with him, learning that he had been severely abused as a child and actually attempted suicide when he was fourteen. Kenny was labeled as "FTA," failure to adapt, and processed for discharge from the Corps.

Although many Marines claimed that attrition was highest when they went through recruit training, it has remained pretty much the same since the 1970s, but there were years when it "spiked" to higher or lower numbers. These spikes were due usually to some new standard being implemented, such as the mandatory drug testing of the early 1980s.

Today's young men or women joining the Corps are slightly different from those in the past. They are the thirteenth generation since the United States was founded, and are larger than any generation coming before at twenty-four-million strong. They also are the most diverse group: ethnically, culturally, and economically. They are more tolerant of differences; they expect diversity in their personal relations. More than half are female, most of whom fully expect to pursue careers.

Although they have a reputation for being lazy, most are crazy about sports and exercise. This is the generation that elevated roller blading, aerobics, and the "Extreme Games" to new national obsessions. Most are in decent physical condition. Their mental toughness was often in question, however, with many quitting during physical training well before reaching their physical limitation.

The explosion in the amount of litigation over the past forty years removed the acceptance of individual responsibility for one's actions. Reliance on the entertainment of television and movies to define appropriate conduct have confused things. Rudeness and unsociable attitudes are celebrated as acceptable wit, and talking back becomes a demonstration of intelligence. The media continues to exploit tabloid news, which tends to sensationalize matters that overshadow values that the Corps feels are truly important. These outside influences blur the boundaries of personal accountability, thus affecting both parent and child. The focus has moved farther and farther from the whole of society and more to the individual—the "me-first" attitude.

Success is tied to material objects, and even "stay in school" advertising campaigns can create an attitude of selfishness. Many feel they've been promised job opportunity with a high school diploma, failing to realize that how one earns the diploma matters. Education is watered down, with separate classes for bright and backward students viewed as elitism, so many are simply forced through the process. The reality of society separating the capable from the inept shocks many and makes some cynical and unwilling to conform.

Typical recruits are often the children of divorced parents. If the parents are married both probably work outside the home. Many young people spend much time home alone after school unsupervised by adults—maybe watched by an older sibling—a generation raising itself. This means that these people tend to be independent, not used to being told what to do and when. Their independence also leads to an inward focus, often demonstrated through individualistic and selfish behavior. The challenge for drill instructors is teaching recruits that they can accomplish more by working as part of a team than as an individual working alone. The type of home life that they were raised in also creates a need for them to find someone with whom they can establish strong emotional bonds, which is an important reason for the drill instructor's role in the Crucible.

Threats of AIDS, drugs, crime, and various other pressures prevent their growing up under the same relaxed conditions as other generations. They did not face a looming and ominous danger that people used to talk about, such as nuclear attack during the cold war. The current dangers are right in their faces and are a part of their everyday life. That causes them to be more callous and less likely to let things frighten them, but more likely to challenge authority. They live in an environment where popular television shows and movies portray many adults having more to learn from children than the reverse. Frequently, they don't believe an elder who tells them that they don't know everything.

Overt challenges to a drill instructor's authority are not unheard of; handling such situations is a tricky matter. Drill instructors' threats of legal action cause recruits to think of complaining to the media or elected officials, to manipulate the situation. While physical abuse is never allowed in any circumstances, it would not be successful for the same reasons.

Some believe that recruits should be slapped around as those in the past say they were. Sergeant Lee had his own thoughts about how much of these stories were fact or exaggeration. In his day as a recruit, although some of his peers would say otherwise, Lee saw only one incident with a recruit that bordered on abuse. It was minor, probably an accident, and the only one. Horrible incidents of abuse happened in the past, but definitely not at the level many people think.

Physical force was not always viewed as abuse in the past. American society was much different a few short decades ago, and such punishment was viewed differently. As one old drill instructor said, "It was never anything more than how I disciplined my sons."

Many of today's recruits have never experienced a spanking as a child, but they have been victims, witnesses, and even the perpetrators of brutally violent crimes, if not in real life, at least in the fantasy of television and movies every evening. Recruiters are sometimes prevented from handing out Marine Corps jackets and T-shirts, because certain colors represent certain gangs and those wearing the color are in threat of attack. To have begun corporal punishment at this point in their lives, when they were adults and Marine Corps recruits, would have been disastrous. Too many already confused violence as manliness.

Because Sergeant Lee had never been struck and knew that he was a good Marine, he saw no use in physically abusing recruits. He was relieved when he arrived at drill-instructor school to learn such abuse was strictly forbidden. Training needs to be tough, but not brutal or sadistic. Those who think otherwise have fallen victim to one of the most common errors of people in leadership positions, that of failing to distinguish between fear and respect. Using fear and intimidation to get results may be successful in some peacetime situations, but once a unit enters combat, things change. Fear and intimidation by a commander cannot compete with that caused by the threats of injury or death from an enemy.

Sergeant Lee knew that if he found himself trapped in a kill zone of a near ambush, he could not use a meek individual with him. The first fifteen to twenty seconds of the firefight would likely determine the outcome, and victory would be dependent on an immediate and ruthlessly violent response. Such a response would not come from individuals willing to be abused because "they thought they deserved it." It requires an instinctive ability to defend oneself and others courageously regardless of the situation.

Today's young men or women want the opportunity to make decisions, but need feedback on their performance to know how they've done. Each recruit will be called on several times to act as the leader during the Crucible. The weak leaders will be forced to lead, and the natural leaders will be forced to follow. Decisions will be made and directions given, but as a group they will sit down with their drill instructor at the end and discuss what was done well and what could have been done better. The basics of problem solving and decision making will be evident and they will clearly see that all actions have consequences. They will also see how the lack of action has its own consequences.

The Crucible assists the drill instructors in overcoming the many challenges they face in training their recruits. It is, however, nothing but a collection of logs and ropes without the human element. Without examining and understanding it, it is easy to mistake the Crucible as just another endurance course. The physical demands are secondary to the emotional effects.

Recruits today are looking for approval and acceptance. Their fear of being forced to do push-ups should be replaced by a dread that their drill instructors will not accept them as fellow Marines. Having the drill instructor take off his campaign cover and treat the recruit differently helps to welcome him to the Corps. The recruit stops viewing the drill instructor as an omnipotent and unapproachable being and starts to look to him as a role model. To experience this transformation under harsh conditions, while reading Medal of Honor citations from Marines of the past, and as part of a team, emphasizes the importance of core values.

The Crucible helps to overcome the recruits' negative traits and in turn helps to transform recruits from citizen-patriots into Marines, a change that will be permanent, regardless of whether they wear the uniform for four years or forty. The obstacles these recruits will overcome in the three days of the Crucible will bond them, and it will let them see that they can do a few things as individuals, but practically anything as a team.

At the end, the drill instructor handing a recruit his first eagle, globe, and anchor will culminate the transformation into a Marine. It creates a sense of belonging that is important to his feeling and acting like a Marine. Then, when the drill instructor puts his campaign cover back on for the last week of training and the treatment stays the same, the recruit, now a new Marine, knows that he or she is truly different. They are more likely to accept the Corps' philosophies—no tolerance of illegal drug use; never to lie, cheat, or steal; and always to treat others with dignity and respect. They are proud of being an accepted member of the Marine Corps.

Already tired from ten miles of hiking, the squad begins crawling through the muck and mud of the endurance course.

As the recruits crawl under a barbed wire obstacle on the day infiltration course, a "casualty" is assessed to increase the stress and friction of the event.

Nearing the end of the day infiltration course, the squad focuses its effort and works as a team to accomplish its mission.

Two recruits work together to drag a heavy ammunition can through a water obstacle on the day infiltration course.

A recruit trips a booby-trap during the day movement portion of the endurance course, causing a second "casualty" for the squad to evacuate.

With just minutes remaining until the time limit on the day movement course, the squad makes it to the ramp of the helicopter with one of the casualties.

In a desperate attempt to complete the day movement course, re-fusing to quit though they have no chance for success, three recruits pull the casualty towards the helicopter.

Two recruits struggle to balance themselves as they pull another man up on to Sgt. Basilone's Challenge.

A recruit jumps for the bar on PFC Garcia's Leap. He knows he won't make it, but trusts that the squad will not let him fall to the ground.

After getting off to a rough start on PFC Jenkins's Pinnacle, the recruits help each other over the unstable log obstacle.

The squad starts out on Sgt. Timmerman's Tank. At first it seems easy, but soon they are frustrated by their failure to use teamwork and move as one entity.

The squad uses empty barrels as pontoons to cross the first station of the reaction course.

Adversity hits the squad as a recruit falls on the second station of the reaction course. Another man falls trying to save him, but a third recruit grabs the valuable board before it is dropped.

With the use of ingenuity and teamwork, the squad pulls a heavy ammunition can on the last station of the reaction course.

Two recruits carefully pull the ammunition can to the top of the obstacle to complete the reaction course.

On PFC Anderson's Fall, a recruit blindly falls backwards from a table into the hands of his comrades.

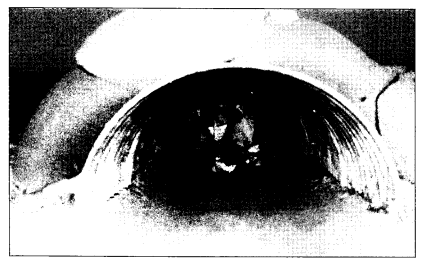

Now nearing 2200 (10 p.m.), after a grueling twenty hour day, a recruit crawls through a culvert on the night infiltration course.

The squad struggles to hang onto the swinging tires of Cpl. Laville's Duty, waiting for one who is having trouble making it across the obstacle.

Near exhaustion after hiking twenty-four miles over the past thirty-four hours with less than four hours of sleep and little food, the squad engages in brutal bouts of close combat on the combat course.

On the last warrior station, LCpl. Noonan's Casualty Evacuation, the squad demonstrates their lessons learned by working together to carry a "wounded" buddy to safety.

6

Sergeant Basilone's Challenge

Early on the morning of 7 December 1941, a sentry at the Marine Barracks, Naval Ammunition Depot, Oahu, made an entry concerning a flight of Japanese airplanes flying toward Schofield Barracks. Minutes later, bombs began falling on Pearl Harbor and the United States entered World War II.

That same morning, Japanese naval gunfire began preparatory fires on the beaches of Midway Island. In China (Tientsin and Peking) small detachments of Marines quickly found themselves surrounded by Japanese soldiers. On 10 December, Japanese infantry landed on the island of Guam and overwhelmed the small Marine garrison.

Japanese warships started firing on Wake Island and its tiny neighbor Wilkes early on 11 December. It was an important piece of coral, because it sat astride the Pacific lines of communication for both the United States and Japan. Marine gunners held their fire, allowing the ships to get close to the island. When they finally opened up on the Japanese flotilla with deadly accuracy, they drove the ships back out to sea. Marine planes then chased them, and by day's end the Japanese would suffer two destroyers sunk, a cruiser and several smaller ships damaged, and several bombers shot down or damaged. The enemy lost more than 500 men, but the Marines had no casualties on Wake. The battle raged for several days, with the 388 Marines fighting heroically against the huge Japanese force that landed on the island. They would inflict more than 1,150 casualties on the enemy before surrendering, unwillingly, on 21 December. Surrender would not come easy, and the Marine commander would need to go to every position personally to get the men to lay down their arms.

67

In 1942, the United States went on the offensive. With a naval victory at Midway in June, the country was ready for a ground battle and victory. Finally, eight months after Pearl Harbor and two months after Midway, the Marines began their first major offensive operation of the war at a place called Guadalcanal.

Guadalcanal was a small island in the Solomon Island chain, less than 600 miles from Japan's huge base on Rabaul. The 1st Marine Division served as the cornerstone for the invasion force, with its ranks of old regulars recently filled out with new recruits:

> They were a motley bunch. Hundreds were young recruits only recently out of boot training at Parris Island. Others were older; first sergeants yanked off the 'planks' in Navy yards, sergeants from recruiting duty, gunnery sergeants who had fought in France, perennial privates with disciplinary records a yard long. These were the professionals, the 'Old Breed' of United States Marines. Many fought *cacos* in Haiti, *banditos* in Nicaragua, and French, English, Italian, and American soldiers and sailors in every bar in Shanghai, Manila, Tsingtao, Tientsin, and Peking.[1]
>
> —Col. Samuel B. Griffith, USMC

On 7 August 1942, Marines hit the beaches of Guadalcanal and the island-hopping campaign began. There was no strong opposition and by the end of the first day, more than 11,000 Marines were deployed on the island and supplies were piling up on the beach. The first amphibious offensive of the war was off to a good start, but the battle would last for six months.

The island's airfield was taken and deemed ready for operations on 12 August. Planes arrived on 15 August and control of the airfield was contended heavily by the enemy, because having air superiority would speed their demise. Fighting in the thick jungles proved to be exhausting and costly. An estimated 23,000 Japanese

1. Moskin, J. Robert, *The U.S. Marine Corps Story*, 3d ed. (New York, McGraw Hill, 1992) 259. Quoting Samuel B. Griffith II, *The Battle for Guadalcanal* (Philadelphia, J. B. Lippincott Co., 1963) 23–24.

were lost, while American Marines and Army troops suffered 1,598 killed and 4,709 wounded before the island was secure on 8 February 1942.

Strategically, the Guagalcanal campaign diverted the Japanese strength by putting them on the defensive, slowing their advance. It was a brutal experience, however, and would prove to be the Marines' longest battle of the war. Marines from "the Canal" were now battle-hardened veterans who could spread their experience throughout the Corps, and their stories of heroism gave the country more hope that America would prevail.

"This obstacle is named after John Basilone of Raritan, New Jersey," Sergeant Lee said. "The son of an Italian immigrant tailor, he was born on 4 November 1916, and was one of ten children. At age eighteen he enlisted in the Army, but after his discharge joined the Marine Corps in 1940. Before World War II he served in Cuba and was serving with 1st Battalion, 7th Marines when he earned the Medal of Honor."

It was 1030 and the recruits were now feeling the effects of their already challenging day, which was, unfortunately, barely one-third complete. The mud from the infiltration and day-movement courses was caked on their uniforms and equipment. They were hot and sweaty, their stomachs were rumbling from lack of food, and their feet hurt from the ten miles they had walked. They were feeling, without a doubt, completely miserable.

The President of the United States in the name of The Congress takes pleasure in presenting the Medal of Honor to Sergeant John Basilone, United States Marine Corps, for service set forth in the following citation:

For extraordinary heroism and conspicuous gallantry in action against enemy Japanese forces, above and beyond the call of duty, while serving with the First Battalion, 7th Marines, 1st Marine Division, in the Lunga Area, Guadalcanal, Solomon Islands, on 24 and 25 October 1942. While the enemy was hammering at the Marines' defensive positions, Sergeant Basilone, in charge of two sections of heavy machine guns, fought valiantly to check the savage and determined assault. In a fierce frontal attack with the Japanese blasting his guns with grenades and mortar fire, one of Sergeant Basilone's sections, with its gun crews, was put out of action, leaving only two men able to carry on. Moving an extra gun into position, he placed it in action, then, under continual fire, repaired another and personally manned it, gallantly holding his line until replacements arrived. A little later with ammunition critically low and the supply lines cut off, Sergeant Basilone, at great risk of his life and in the face of continued enemy attack, battled his way through hostile lines with urgently needed shells for his gunners, thereby contributing in large measure to the virtual annihilation of a Japanese regiment. His great personal valor and courageous initiative were in keeping with the highest traditions of the United States Naval Service. Signed, Franklin D. Roosevelt[2]

Sergeant Lee looked around at the squad before choosing a leader for this obstacle. He didn't want to ask for a volunteer again, because it was important to get all of the recruits involved in acting as the leader. The weaker recruits would likely end up in charge during the last few events if the drill instructors didn't force them to step forward now. They would be the most tired toward the end of the Crucible, when a strong leader would most be needed, making things even more difficult for a weaker recruit. Participating usually helps a recruit to break out of his shell also, so it was important that they not wait until the end. If a recruit were successful during his session as the unit leader, it would be a huge boost to his motivation and willingness to participate.

"Mascuzzio, you're the leader," said Sergeant Lee, surprising him by the sudden thrust into a position of authority.

Mascuzzio was immature and had difficulty getting along with his fellow recruits. He joined to fulfill a lifelong dream of becoming a

2. Medal of Honor citation from *The Congressional Medal of Honor, The Names, The Deeds* (Chico, Calif., Sharp and Dunnigan, 1988) 256.

Marine, and planned on marrying his high school sweetheart after recruit training. This was a real mistake in Sergeant Lee's opinion, feeling that a Marine should not marry until he or she was at least twenty-five, became a corporal, and had known the prospective spouse for two years. When he asked recruits why they wanted to marry at such a young age, and with the challenge of military service in front of them, the only answer was often *'cause I'm in love, sir.* Mascuzzio was having enough trouble taking care of himself, so his new marriage would probably not last as long as his first hitch in the Corps.

"This is the situation: While conducting operations in a city your platoon has come under sniper fire. You were crossing a street when the gunfire erupted. Your squad was left on the far side of the street from your platoon. You discovered a route behind a building that will reunite you with your platoon, but there is a barbed-wire fence blocking the way. You notice a fallen telephone pole over one portion of the fence," The obstacle was constructed with three large logs. Two vertical logs were placed twenty feet apart and held a horizontal log about eight feet from the ground, resembling the frame of a soccer goal, something for recruits to climb over. Sergeant Lee pointed at the horizontal log, which symbolized the pole. "You have the spare ammunition for the automatic weapons, located with the platoon, which is now under heavy enemy fire. Your mission is to cross over the barbed-wire fence using the downed telephone pole and resupply your platoon's automatic-weapon teams. You will wear your helmet and load-bearing vest and pass your rifle over the obstacle. You have to carry that ammunition," Sergeant Lee pointed to yet another set of ammunition cans full of dirt.

"Coordinating instructions: One, do not touch the vertical support logs. Two, two spotters will be placed on each side of the obstacle, prepared to catch any falling recruit. Three, do not lift recruits by their load-bearing vests. Four, do not throw anything over the beam. Before you take action, you must brief me on your plan. Are there any questions?"

Mascuzzio was obviously overwhelmed, still reeling from the shock of being put in charge. "What are we supposed to do, Sergeant?"

Lee's instincts were telling him to revert back to the first few days of training and begin a tongue lashing that Mascuzzio would not soon forget, but that would have been the wrong example to set. Making the man feel stupid because he was not a natural leader would not make him better. It was his responsibility to train Mascuzzio, to make him better, to make him into a Marine.

"You, the squad, and all of this gear are going over that log," Sergeant Lee pointed to the beam again. "Main thing, don't use the vertical logs for support."

Mascuzzio turned around to face the squad. The silence was almost painful. Remembering what the other leaders had done, Mascuzzio muttered, "Any ideas?" Fortunately, many of the squad members had some good suggestions on how they should accomplish their mission, so Mascuzzio was able to pick ideas from the others.

Combining two suggested plans, Mascuzzio briefed Sergeant Lee and the squad started to work. Mascuzzio was having obvious difficulty but the point of the Crucible was not to make every individual into an exceptional leader. All would need to be capable of leading if the need arose, but these men would soon be the juniormost Marines in the Corps and would need to follow before they ever had such a chance.

After the squad boosted two recruits up onto the log, and a third to the other side, the men began moving the ammunition cans over the obstacle. Next, the weaker recruits were sent; the squad had already learned that those who might have problems should go first. More and more, however, Simms began to dominate the squad and take charge. Mascuzzio stepped aside and let him, making it seem as if Simms were actually the squad leader.

"Hello there, fourth squad," snapped Sergeant Lee. "Who is in charge?" No one said anything, but they all looked at Mascuzzio. "Well?"

"I am, Sergeant," said Mascuzzio.

"So why are you doing everything, Simms? Part of being a good leader is having the ability to be a good follower. You're always going to have a boss. Even the commandant answers to the secretaries of the Navy and Defense, the Congress, and the president. Take charge, Mascuzzio; you can no longer speak, Simms."

Situations like this came up occasionally. A natural leader dominates, and the best way to handle it is to point out the problem, and silence or "kill" him. It was a delicate balance between discouraging initiative and allowing everyone to have the opportunity to lead.

The majority of the squad was soon on the other side, with just Mascuzzio left. Getting him over proved to be extremely difficult, because the mud all over his uniform made him slip off the vertical log every time he jumped up to grab it. The two recruits balancing themselves on the log were also unstable and unable to provide enough help to get Mascuzzio over. He was getting tired and would soon lack the energy to make a worthy attempt. One of the recruits got on his hands and knees so Simms could stand on him, providing a third set of hands to grab Mascuzzio. Simms was able to stabilize him on the log, while the other two pulled and fought to inch him higher and higher on the obstacle. Finally, Mascuzzio was balanced on top and able to swing over the log to join the rest of the squad on the other side. With only a few hours of the Crucible under their belts, the recruits were already learning how to work well together as a team.

"What did you do right?" asked Sergeant Lee after circling the recruits for the debrief.

"We worked well together, even better than before," said Nushi.

"What wasn't done very well?"

"I was too bossy, I didn't let Mascuzzio have his turn," said Simms.

"Tell me how you think it went, Mascuzzio," said Sergeant Lee.

"Well, I have to admit that I wasn't comfortable being the leader, but I also know that all good Marines step forward and take charge when a leader is needed."

"And you did that. Don't think you did a lousy job, because you recognized that the others could offer suggestions that would help you, right?"

"Yes, Sergeant."

"The most important part is that you took charge. Selecting the leadership style you're going to use depends on the situation. You came up with a plan and executed it."

"Well, actually, I used a combination of two of the other recruits' plans," said Mascuzzio.

"And that's okay. You accessed the situation, asked for input, and made a decision based on the advice of your buddies, right?"

"Yes, Sergeant."

"But then things got a little out of hand when it came time for execution and you lost control as the leader."

"I just didn't feel comfortable, Sergeant. I guess it takes a special type of person to lead," said Mascuzzio.

"It doesn't take anything more than what we've taught you during boot camp. What was special about Gunnery Sergeant Basilone?" asked Sergeant Lee.

"He didn't quit," said a recruit.

"What else?" asked Sergeant Lee. "He did more than that, right?"

The recruits didn't answer. They were starting to get tired, the adrenaline generated by the last obstacle was beginning to lapse. Sergeant Lee would need to strike a nerve to bring them back to where he wanted them.

"Let me read what one of his buddies said, 'Basilone had a machine gun on the go for three days and nights without sleep, rest, or food.' How was he able to do that?"

"Courage, Sergeant," said Simms.

"Right, what else?"

"Dedication, Sergeant," said Mascuzzio.

"Anything else?"

"Discipline, Sergeant," said Nushi.

"Not only discipline, but *self*-discipline, right?" The recruits nodded in agreement. "He held himself responsible for the operation of that machine gun because he knew that it was important to his fellow Marines and his mission. He had the self-discipline to continually clean and maintain the machine gun so it would operate properly. Meticulous attention to detail was necessary, just like the attention to detail you had to put into preparing for an inspection, right?"

"Yes, Sergeant."

"For Basilone to do this he had to neglect his own needs to concentrate on doing his duty. He was a very rare person. Does anyone else know what's so special about John Basilone?"

"He was the first enlisted Marine to win the Medal of Honor during World War II," said Simms.

"That's right, as you learned in your history class. But that's not what I'm looking for, and besides you don't really *win* something like the Medal of Honor. It's not a contest, you *earn* it through heroic actions. Can anyone else tell me why he was so courageous?"

The recruits said nothing.

"He received the Navy Cross, too, our second-highest award for valor. After he returned from Guadalcanal, they tried to make him into an officer but he chose to stay enlisted. In July 1944 he married a sergeant in the women's reserve named Lena Riggi, right out here in Oceanside." Sergeant Lee pointed off to the south and looked at Mascuzzio. "Think about it: He was twenty-eight, a gunnery sergeant, and recipient of the Medal of Honor before he got married.

"On 19 February 1945, Basilone landed with the three Marine divisions that assaulted Iwo Jima. He was fighting hard, leading his machine-gun platoon forward against Japanese forces in caves and fortified positions. When they came to an enemy strong point, he climbed up on a blockhouse and attacked it with grenades and demolition charges. Then under intense fire, he guided a tank through a minefield before being mortally wounded by a mortar round."

"Did he have to go back and fight, after earning the Medal of Honor, and all?" asked Smith.

"No, he just wanted to continue to serve," said Sergeant Lee. "Marines just always seem to amaze me. I just can't believe that there is a finer group; I've met the greatest people in the world in the Corps. On one of my deployments there was even a pilot who had lost his arm in Grenada but was still a serving Marine.[3] He's now a lientenant colonel and he still passes the PFT and qualifies with his weapon. Why would a Marine do this?"

Because "Marines take care of each other," said Smith. "He wants to stay a Marine."

"And it's up to all of you to continue, whether it's on the battlefield or here in the States."

3. Three helicopter pilots gave their lives protecting him after he was shot down: Captain John P. Gigueve, Jeb F. Seagle, and 1st Lt. Jeffery R. Scharver. Their action made it possible for another helo to land and save him.

7

Private First Class Garcia's Leap

On Sunday, 25 June 1950, several divisions of the North Korean People's Army crossed the thirty-eighth parallel into South Korea and countries all over the world joined with the United Nations forces to protect South Korea. General Douglas MacArthur, the new commander in chief of United Nations forces, immediately requested a Marine air-ground brigade, and the 1st Provisional Brigade at Camp Pendleton began to pack to go to war. Lieutenant General Lemuel Shepard of the Marine Corps was sent to confer with MacArthur in Japan and jumped on his comment, "If only I had the 1st Marine Division . . ." Shepard told MacArthur that he could plan on having them by September. The Corps was only 74,000 strong, but they would grow, again, to more than 260,000 before hostilities ceased three years later.

On 12 July 1950, only seventeen days after North Korea crossed the border, the Marine Brigade sailed from San Diego's port. They were sent directly into action on the Pusan Perimeter, a thin defensive position that only encompassed a few hundred square miles. It was the last bit of Korea held by the Allies, and the Marines were MacArthur's last available reserve.

The Marines landed in Korea on 2 August, and were sent to one of the most vulnerable locations on the perimeter. The August heat made conditions unbearable with temperatures sometimes rising above 110 degrees. After several small-unit clashes, Marines were ordered to counterattack the enemy at the Naktong bulge, a natural approach on the western side of the Allied lines and along a river. A British military observer reported:

If Miryang is lost Taegu becomes untenable and we will be faced with a withdrawal from Korea. I am heartened that the Marine Brigade will move against the Naktong Salient tomorrow. They are faced with impossible odds, and I have no valid reason to substantiate it, but I have the feeling they will halt the enemy . . . These Marines have a swagger, confidence, and hardness that must have been in Stonewall Jackson's Army of the Shenandoah. They remind me of the Coldstreams at Dunkirk. Upon this thin line of reasoning, I cling to the hope of victory.[1]

With Marine infantry and air working together in perfect coordination, the North Korean Army was forced back across the Naktong River. Pressure on the Pusan Perimeter would reduce, but the allied forces did not have the resources to launch a large counterattack from Pusan. To gain the offensive it was going to be necessary to attack the enemy's flank in his overextended supply line. The Marines were called on again.

By mid-August, sufficient reservists and replacements from various posts filled out the 1st Marine Division's ranks, allowing it to set sail for Korea at near its authorized combat strength. Its destination was a landing at Inchon, on the west coast of South Korea. The landing itself was precarious because of dramatic changes in tide conditions and hazardous mud flats. The Marines would first need to attack the small island of Wolmi-do, which dominated the inner harbor on the morning tide, and then attack the mainland on the evening tide. The hours in between would leave the Marines on the island stranded and vulnerable to enemy counterattack.

The division at sea was joined by the Marines from the Pusan Perimeter in early September. They landed at Inchon on 15 September, taking the first objective of Wolmi-do Island by 0800. They met scattered resistance and quickly blocked the causeway leading to Inchon. As the American flag rose, General MacArthur said,

1. Moskin, J. Robert, *The U.S. Marine Corps Story*, 3d ed. (New York, McGraw Hill, 1992) 453. Quoting Andrew Geer, *The New Breed: The Story of U.S. Marines in Korea* (New York, Harper & Bros., 1952) 10–11.

"That's it, let's get a cup of coffee," and then sent a message to the fleet: "The Navy and Marines have never shone more brightly than this morning."[2]

On Wolmi-do the Marines dug in and waited the eight hours for the tides to change so the second phase of the operation could begin. At 1730, coxswains rammed their landing craft into the seawalls of Inchon and Marines used wooden ladders to climb into the port city. The currents pushed some Marines two miles from their intended landing beach, but they quickly organized and moved forward.

Enemy forces were shocked by the amphibious attack. The 1st Marine Division secured Inchon and fought its way up the highway into Seoul. The fighting proved to be brutal; barricade-to-barricade, street-to-street, and house-to-house. But, as expected, the division accomplished its mission. The entire landing was executed with daring and speed, and Seoul was retaken in less than two weeks. The enemy suffered more than 13,000 casualties and the Marines had 421 killed and more than 2,000 wounded. The back of the North Korean Army was broken and the Eighth Army attacked north from Pusan, coordinating its counteroffensive with the Marines of IX Corps.

On 9 October, U.S. forces crossed the thirty-eighth parallel and the war took on a whole new life. Allied troops encountered the Chinese People's Liberation Army near the Yalu River, but intelligence estimates doubted that the Chinese would become involved in a full-scale war.

On 26 October, the 1st Marine Division began another amphibious landing at the North Korean city of Wonsan, located on the east coast of Korea and more than 100 miles north of the thirty-eighth parallel. Sea mines delayed the landing for sixteen days, and the great American Bob Hope was already performing with his USO show by the time the Marines landed. They moved farther north and

2. Moskin, J. Robert, *The U.S. Marine Corps Story*, 3d ed. (New York, Mc-Graw Hill, 1992) 465. Quoting Lynn Montross and Nicholas Canzona, *U.S. Marine Operations in Korea*, vol. 2: *The Inchon-Seoul Operation* (Arlington, Headquarters, USMC, 1955) 92–93.

by mid-November they arrived at the Chosin Reservoir, 125 miles south of the Chinese border. In bitter cold weather, the 1st Marine Division found itself surrounded by eight divisions of Chinese troops. On 27 November, the Chinese attacked elements of the 7th Marine Regiment. The Marines suffered heavy casualties, but fought off the larger force in a night full of brutal warfare. Hell finally froze over, and Marines would forever call it the *Frozen Chosin.*

On 30 November, the Marines were ordered to move south to attempt a breakout of the Chosin position. The situation seemed hopeless: stranded in the frozen wasteland, tragically outnumbered and encircled. "Those poor bastards! They've got us right where we want 'em. We can shoot in every direction now,"[3] said Col. Lewis "Chesty" Puller when he was asked if he knew his regiment was surrounded.

The fighting withdrawal began on 1 December and would last for two horrific weeks. Marines brought out their wounded and dead along with shattered Army units as well as their salvaged vehicles and equipment. The battle would be extremely bloody, with Chesty Puller's 1st Marine Regiment fighting a brave rearguard action through the frozen hills that virtually destroyed seven of the Chinese divisions. During the Chosin campaign, 719 Marines were killed, 3,508 were wounded, and at least 7,313 were nonbattle casualties, mostly from frostbite.

With the Chinese in the fight a bitter standstill began. The war would become a static conflict of outpost warfare, categorized by bloody and costly clashes that gained little ground. When the fighting finally ended in mid-July 1953, forty-two Marines had received the Medal of Honor and more than 4,500 had given their lives.

The Corps made huge strides forward during the Korean War. For the first time, Marines demonstrated the effectiveness of helicopters on the battlefield. Also, when the Department of Defense and Congress investigated and admonished other services for the poor performance of U.S. troops as prisoners of war in Korea, they praised the Marines for their loyalty under extreme psychological and phys-

3. Davis, Burke, *Marine! The Life of Chesty Puller* (Boston, Little, Brown and Company, Inc., 1962) 2.

ical torture. The Corps proved that it was still an elite and courageous fighting organization that could be counted on as the nation's force in readiness.

"This obstacle is named in honor of Fernando L. Garcia of San Juan, Puerto Rico," read Sergeant Lee. It was 1110, forty-four hours and fifty minutes to go. "Born on 14 October 1929, at Utuado, Puerto Rico, Garcia was working as a file clerk before joining the Marine Corps in September of 1951. By March of 1952, Garcia completed recruit training, infantry training, and was sent to Korea.

The President of the United States in the name of The Congress takes pleasure in presenting the Medal of Honor posthumously to Private First Class Fernando L. Garcia, United States Marine Corps, for service set forth in the following citation:

> For conspicuous gallantry and intrepidity at the risk of his life above and beyond the call of duty while serving as a member of Company I, 3d Battalion, 5th Marines, 1st Marine Division (Rein), in action against enemy aggressor forces in Korea [on 5 September 1952]. While participating in the defense of a combat outpost located more than one mile forward of the main line of resistance during a savage night attack by a fanatical enemy force employing grenades, mortars, and artillery, Private first class Garcia, although suffering painful wounds, moved through the intense hail of hostile fire to a supply point to secure more hand grenades. Quick to act when a hostile grenade landed nearby, endangering the life of another Marine, as well as his own, he unhesitatingly chose to sacrifice himself and immediately threw his body upon the deadly missile, receiving the full impact of the explosion. His great personal valor and cool decision in the face of almost certain death sustain and enhance the finest traditions of the U.S. Naval Service. He gallantly gave his life for his country. Signed, Dwight D. Eisenhower[4]

4. Medal of Honor citation from *The Congressional Medal of Honor, The Names, The Deeds* (Chico, Calif., Sharp and Dunnigan, 1988) 193.

Sergeant Lee looked around the squad, "Who wants to be the squad leader?" he asked.

"I will, Sergeant," said Recruit Waters, surprising everyone in the squad.

Waters was a little different from the others. The senior drill instructor, Staff Sergeant Macias, called him the most improved recruit he'd seen in more than two years as a drill instructor, but Sergeant Lee thought that he was also one of the worst recruits ever. He'd joined to prove to himself and everyone else that he could succeed at something. True, he had made amazing progress, but that was due more to the fact that he was completely screwed up when he arrived, than his becoming squared away. He broke down in the first week of training and had to be sent to see the lieutenant. The series commander questioned Waters about wanting to hurt himself or others, prodding to determine if he might be a suicide risk, but Waters just looked at him as if he were crazy. He couldn't even imagine trying to hurt himself; he just wanted to leave the Marine Corps.

Waters was shaking uncontrollably, saying, "I just want to go home." The lieutenant just said, "Nope, you're staying here with me," and sent him back to the platoon. Waters's reaction was not uncommon. Most recruits would quickly go home during the first two or three weeks if given the opportunity. Waters would probably be a good Marine, but would probably never be a top performer.

Sergeant Lee said, "While crossing a bridge, your squad came under enemy air attack. There were no casualties, but the bridge was damaged, leaving a gap between two parts of the bridge. A member of your squad is on the far side. Some posts remain by the gap, as well as some cables suspended over the hole."

The obstacle consisted of a vertical bar suspended about ten feet off the ground by two cables hung on a log frame. About fifteen feet from the vertical bar there was a post, resembling a tree stump, protruding two feet above the ground.

"Your mission is to reunite the separated team member with your squad and continue the mission. He will be at the post. Everyone else will be under the bar, and you're not going to wear any gear.

"Coordinating instructions: One, team members under the bar will line up facing each other, with their arms extended. Two, the man on the post must jump for the bar, trying to touch it, but not grabbing it. Are there any questions?"

"Will all of us take turns jumping?" asked Waters.

"Of course," answered Sergeant Lee. "Everyone will jump, and the rest of us will catch him."

There wasn't any planning needed for this obstacle because there was only one way to do it. Being the leader, Waters tried to get up on the log to jump first, but was stopped by Sergeant Lee. "I'm first, you're going to have to go after me, Waters."

"You're going to jump, Sergeant?" asked Waters.

"If that's all right with you," said Sergeant Lee sarcastically. "Now let's talk for a second, fourth squad." Lee was standing on top of the post smiling, "Let's forget about all the time I've ITed you during the past three months, huh?"

The recruits laughed. They were lined up in two rows, facing each other so they could catch him before he fell to the ground.

"Let's forget about all the times I've made your life miserable, and found joy in your pity—*GOOD TO GO?*"

"*YES, SERGEANT!*"

"*JUMPER JUMPER!*" yelled Sergeant Lee.

"*JUMP AWAY!*" sounded the squad and Sergeant Lee jumped out toward the bar. He came close but didn't touch it, falling into the hands of the recruits.

"Well, you can put me down now!" said Sergeant Lee as the squad laughed again. Each of the recruits then took a turn getting on the log and jumping for the bar. Only one touched it, and all jumped knowing that there was no way they would be able to actually grab the bar. Their fate was in the hands, literally, of their brother recruits. Even the recruits who had some fear of heights jumped without hesitation. The example of their drill instructor was enough to make their fear mean little, because they wanted more than anything to be just like him.

The obstacle required enormous trust in the squad members, because the jump was hopeless and there was no chance that one would grab the bar. The commitment of the squad to each of the individual members was reminiscent of Private First Class Garcia's commitment to his buddy. The apprehension that each recruit may have had before jumping, knowing that he could not touch the bar, paled in comparison to the feelings Garcia must have had when he jumped on the grenade, knowing he would probably die.

"Pretty easy stuff?" asked Sergeant Lee.

"Yes, Sergeant," said the recruits.

"How did you feel when you jumped, Waters?"

"I knew I wasn't going to make it, but I knew I was safe."

"Why did he feel safe?"

"Because we were going to catch him," said Smith, "he trusted us."

"How do you think Garcia felt when he jumped on that grenade?" The recruits were silent; the fun was gone. "You know, when he jumped, he yelled, 'I got it!' Can you believe that it was that deliberate an act?"

"I can't even imagine it, Sergeant," said Simms.

"Which core value was he demonstrating by his actions?"

"Courage," said a recruit.

"Actually, probably all of them, Sergeant," answered Waters. "He was courageous, committed, and had to have a lot of honor."

"He did what he did knowing that he would die," said Mascuzzio.

"Well, in some ways, we get paid to die," said a recruit.

"Who the heck taught you that?" snapped Sergeant Lee.

"I . . . no one, Sergeant."

"That's nothing but BS, you understand me?"

"YES, SERGEANT," sounded the squad.

"Don't let anyone tell you that you get paid to die. You're going through three months of boot camp so you don't die. So you make the enemy die for his cause. You are trained to *fight*, not die! Do we practice diving on grenades?"

"NO, SERGEANT," sounded the squad.

"That's why what Garcia did was so amazing. Not only did he ignore his natural instincts of survival, but he also disregarded all of his training, and for what?"

"For another Marine."

"There was no political rhetoric; no debate whether it's a 'right' or 'wrong' war. He ignored human instincts of survival and his training to protect brother Marines. A few of the warrior stations are named after Marines who shielded others from grenades, but don't think for one second that we are training you to do the same. We use them as examples because they made the ultimate sacrifice."

"What would you do in that situation, Sergeant?" asked a recruit.

"How can I honestly answer that? I might be able to speculate on what I would like to think I would do, but I would be cheapening what Private First Class Garcia did if I tried to stand here and say I could do it, too. I just don't think you know till you're there, faced with the situation."

8

Private First Class Jenkins's Pinnacle

On any military scale, the North Vietnamese offensive during the Tet holiday February 1968 was an overwhelming victory for the United States and South Vietnamese forces. The communists gained no new territory, lost more than 15,000 soldiers, and murdered many thousands of civilians. But as Lt. Gen. Lewis Walt of the U.S. Marines said, "This is first a political war, second a psychological war, and third a military war."[1] The fact that the communists were even able to launch the attack in the first place amounted to a political defeat for the American forces.

Robert McNamara became even more disillusioned with the war, and Clark Clifford replaced him as the secretary of defense on 1 March 1968. On 22 March, President Johnson suddenly replaced General Westmoreland with General Abrams as commander, Military Assistance Command, Vietnam. On 31 March, Johnson halted the bombing of North Vietnam, except near the DMZ (demilitarized zone) to get peace talks started. Then he announced that he would not seek reelection in the 1968 campaign. In the end, Hue was recaptured, but Tet-related battles around Khe Sanh would continue until April 1968.

Khe Sanh was located less than twenty miles south of the DMZ, and was originally occupied by Marines during a battalion-sized helicopter assault in late 1966. Since then, the Marine presence had

1. Alexander, Joseph H., *A Fellowship of Valor: The Battle History of the United States Marines* (New York, HarperCollins, 1997) 315.

grown into a firebase and airfield defended by much of the 26th Marine Regiment. Intelligence reports indicated that two enemy divisions were closing in on the base by late 1967, but the Marine command decided to continue to defend the isolated outpost. In fact, there was little room for any other choice. The road out was closed, so the only way for the Marines to be evacuated was by air. They would have been forced to leave an enormous amount of equipment and supplies at the base for the enemy. Defending Khe Sanh thus was the only logical decision.

This course of action was controversial, with President Johnson requiring the Joint Chiefs of Staff to confirm in writing that the base would not fall and become an American Dien Bien Phu. It did not, because the Marines fought with the same determined will displayed by their predecessors at Belleau Wood, Guadalcanal, and the Chosin Reservoir.

Increased enemy activity in January 1968 led to the base being reinforced. By the time the siege began on 21 January, the defending force, consisting of four Marine battalions, one Vietnamese ranger battalion, tanks, and artillery numbered more than 6,000 men. With the road closed, reinforcements, supplies, and casualties had to come in and go out by air. Once again the Marines were surrounded and outnumbered by an enemy, and once again the enemy would pay for the mistake.

The enemy increased the pressure on the base with classic siege tactics, digging concentric trenches around the base and hitting the defenders with up to 1,000 mortar and artillery rounds daily. The Marines countered with everything the regiment could muster, and numerous air strikes, including B-52 bombers. More than 100,000 tons of bombs and 150,000 artillery rounds smashed into the North Vietnamese troops trying to overrun Khe Sanh.

The siege finally ended on 30 March, after seventy-seven bloody days. There were 205 Marines killed and more than 1,600 wounded, but the two divisions attacking the Marines suffered more than 10,000 dead. The 9th Marine Regiment worked its way up the reopened highway in early April and the battle ended soon afterward.

Marines pushed the remaining communist battalions back across the DMZ and reorganized defenses to allow for more mobile operations. They returned to their preferred pacification operations, and by the end of 1968 there were four battalion-sized combined-action groups. As the year closed, more than 85,000 Marines were in country and the heroism of fifty-one Marines in Vietnam had been recognized by the Medal of Honor. Many were earned by young Marines, not even old enough to legally drink in their hometown, while trying to protect buddies.

"The obstacle your squad is about to complete is named in honor of Robert H. Jenkins Jr." It was finally noon, and even though the Crucible was now ten hours old, the day wasn't even half complete. Even worse, it would continue for another forty-four hours. "Jenkins was from Interlachen, Florida. He was born on 1 June 1948 and joined the Marine Corps in February of 1968. After recruit training and infantry training he was sent to Vietnam in late May 1968.

The President of the United States in the name of The Congress takes pleasure in presenting the Medal of Honor posthumously to Private First Class Robert H. Jenkins Jr., United States Marine Corps, for service set forth in the following citation:

For conspicuous gallantry and intrepidity at the risk of his life above and beyond the call of duty while serving as a machine gunner with Company C, 3d Reconnaissance Battalion, 3d Marine Division in connection with operations against enemy forces. Early in the morning of [5 March 1969] Private first class Jenkins's twelve-man reconnaissance team was occupying a defensive position at Fire Support Base Argonne south of the Demilitarized Zone. Suddenly, the Marines were assaulted by a North Vietnamese Army platoon employing mortars, automatic weapons, and hand grenades. Reacting instantly, Private first class Jenkins and another Marine quickly moved into a two-man fighting emplacement, and as they boldly delivered accurate machine-gun fire against the enemy a North Vietnamese soldier threw a hand grenade into the friendly emplacement. Fully realizing the inevitable results of his actions, Private first class Jenkins quickly seized his comrade, and pushing the man to the ground, he leaped on top of the Marine to shield him from the explosion. Absorbing the full impact of the detonation, Private first class Jenkins was seriously injured and subsequently succumbed to his wounds. His courage, inspiring valor, and selfless devotion to duty saved a fellow Marine from serious injury or possible death, and upheld the highest traditions of the Marine Corps and the U.S. Naval Service. He gallantly gave his life for his country. Signed, Richard M. Nixon[2]

"Who wants the honor of being the squad leader for this one?" asked Sergeant Lee, but before anyone could answer he pointed to a recruit. "Good, you're it, Hill."

Hill would never be labeled as the best Marine in the unit, but he would not be a burden on any command either. He enlisted because the Marine Corps would guarantee a military occupation specialty (MOS) associated with aircraft. He joined from rural North Dakota because he didn't want to spend the rest of his life waking up at 0330 to milk the cows. As silly as it might sound, his decision to join the Corps was out of a desire to make life simpler. Another motivating fact was that the Marine Corps brought opportunities for excitement and world travel.

"During an amphibious assault your landing boat ran aground on a sand bar just short of the beach." Sergeant Lee pointed to the obstacle. "The water is too deep to exit over the sides of the boat, but to the front it is only waist deep. A sailor has constructed a ladder to scale the front of the boat. You have those ammunition cans," he pointed to the sand-filled canisters, "needed for your platoon's assault on the beach. Questions, so far?"

In front of the recruits there was an awkward and unstable-looking set of logs. The first log was about five feet from the ground, with the second another five feet up, ten feet above the ground. The two were suspended by cables hanging from a log frame. The cables allowed it to swing back and forth like a child's swing set.

"No, Sergeant," said Hill.

"Your mission is to climb over the front of the boat, using the

---

2. Medal of Honor citation from *The Congressional Medal of Honor, The Names, The Deeds* (Chico, Calif., Sharp and Dunnigan, 1988) 81.

hastily constructed ladder and resupply your platoon with ammunition for the assault. You will wear your helmets and load-bearing vests, and pass your rifles over the obstacle.

"Coordinating instructions: One, recruits on the ground may not steady the logs. Two, recruits will be placed on each side of the obstacle to catch someone who falls. Three, do not use the cables to help you climb. Four, all recruits and gear must go over the top beam. Five, do not use the upright poles. Six, no more than two recruits will be on the obstacle at any given time. Questions?"

"No, Sergeant," said Hill.

"Well, then get to it, tell me when you have a plan."

Hill collected the squad in a huddle and gave instructions. There was very little talk from any of the others.

"We're ready to brief you now, Sergeant," said Hill after a minute.

"Let me hear it."

Hill explained how he was going to go over the obstacle first and demonstrate to the others the best way to complete it. The others would then follow one at a time.

"And you all agreed on this?" asked Sergeant Lee.

"Yes, Sergeant," sounded the recruits, a little dubious. At least most of them did. Some obviously were a little concerned about their own ability to get over the obstacle, but were too apprehensive to say anything. Sergeant Lee considered changing the plan to ensure the recruits utilized teamwork, but decided he'd let them make the mistake so they could learn from it.

Hill was naturally agile and had good balance, making manipulation of the unstable ladder look easy. He jumped on the first log, causing it to swing, but soon stabilized himself. Cautiously he stood to grab the second log, swinging his feet over it almost with the same motion one would use to mount a horse. Several other recruits made it over by themselves with little difficulty, but soon there were problems with the recruits carrying the ammunition cans. They fell or failed to make it up and over the ladder. There was some discussion of how they could resort to teamwork, but Hill kept saying, "just listen to me," as he tried to explain how each recruit could get over on his own.

"Stop!" said Sergeant Lee. "Let's think about what we're friggin' doing here. Marines didn't raise the flag on Mount Suribachi by being a bunch of individuals. Regardless of whether or not everyone can do it on his own, we can do it a lot better and a lot faster by using teamwork."

Hill saw that he was making a mistake, so he placed one recruit on the ladder to help the others. First, they handed over all the ammunition cans. An obvious need, but one originally overlooked by the tired recruits. Then they started helping each other over the ladder and were soon done. It became an easy obstacle when teamwork was used.

"Was this easier or harder when we worked together as a team?" asked Sergeant Lee.

"Much easier as a team," said Hill.

"Yes, Sergeant," said Smith, "we needed to help those who might have had a difficult time on this."

"Why is it important to know the individual abilities of team members?"

"So we know what we can do to help each other, Sergeant," said Waters. "That way we can overcome individual weaknesses by using the team's strengths."

Waters had a tendency to surprise Sergeant Lee and the other drill instructors. His response was remarkably perceptive, as was an answer he had made during marksmanship training. When asked what the most important part of the rifle was, Waters thought for a second and then said, "the Marine using it." No one taught him that; he came up with the correct conclusion entirely on his own. Lieutenant Harris proclaimed, jokingly, away from the recruits' hearing, that Waters was a genius and they were all idiots.

"That's absolutely right, Waters. Why didn't you do that, Hill?"

"I was thinking that it would be better if everyone learned to accomplish the obstacle on his own. That way each recruit would be more confident if he knew he was capable of doing it himself."

"There's some validity to that. We don't want to carry everybody and baby someone into dependence, but this is not the time or the place to be trying to beef up everyone's confidence. We're on the Crucible; you have a mission. Save that type of stuff for the appropriate time, like training. Why didn't anyone say anything, though? Didn't you know you were going to have problems, Smith?"

"Yes, but I . . . I just didn't say anything," said Smith. "I was worried what the others might think if I said I couldn't do it."

"What does it take to speak up when necessary, especially when given an opportunity?"

"The courage to do what is right, Sergeant," said Smith.

"Moral courage, and what about when you're going over the ladder? How did you feel when you crossed over the top plank—especially the first man over?"

"A little scared that I was going to come crashing down on my head, Sergeant," said Hill.

"What kind of courage is that when you keep going, though?" said Sergeant Lee.

"Physical courage, Sergeant," said Simms.

"Overcoming fear, regardless of whether it's moral or physical, to do your duty, and to be loyal to your fellow Marines, right?"

"Yes, Sergeant."

"How was Private first class Jenkins loyal to his fellow Marines?"

"Well, he actually demonstrated loyalty that was way past what was required of his duty," said Smith.

"He knowingly sacrificed his life for his fellow Marines," said Simms. "He wouldn't have won, I mean received, the Medal of Honor if it was just his duty."

"That's right, but how did he help the squad?"

"From when he saved the life of the Marine in the hole with him," said Hill.

"Yes, again, but how did he help the entire squad?"

"When he sacrificed his life he saved the life of a Marine who was manning a machine gun," said Waters. "If the grenade would have killed or wounded them both, then the squad would have been without that machine gun."

"There were only twelve of them," said a recruit, "so it's pretty safe to guess that could have been the end of the entire squad."

"They were under attack by a platoon using mortars and machine guns," said Sergeant Lee. "They were already outgunned and outnumbered, so they would have been in a lot of trouble without that machine gun. I just wonder sometimes if Private first class Jenkins knew that when he died. I wonder if he had enough time to consciously think that if he didn't throw himself on the Marine, all of his buddies would die. Our platoon might need this ammunition that you were toting as much as that squad needed that machine gun. That's why it's important that we use teamwork to go over the obstacle fast, rather than take the longer route as individuals."

"Doing what we were trained to do: work together," said Mascuzzio.

"Private first class Jenkins could have worried about himself and jumped in the other direction rather than protect the other Marine," said Simms.

"He might have saved himself if he weren't so worried about the other guy."

"Reminds me of a great story about American warriors," said Sergeant Lee. "From when, or I guess really *why*, I went to Somalia. I was on a MEU(SOC)[3] deployment in October 1993, when the Army Rangers did their raid to try and capture a Somali warlord. The Rangers fought bravely in some of the most brutal combat involving Americans since the Vietnam War, with eighteen soldiers killed, and two receiving the Medal of Honor. We were sent there after, to sit off the coast in case more forces were needed.

"Earlier that day, a vehicle carrying three Marines was blown up by a command-detonated mine. All were hurt and dazed by the explosion, but two could have easily made it safely to a nearby Army camp. The problem was that the third, a Marine warrant officer, was badly hurt and trapped in the vehicle. With small-arms rounds impacting around them, a sergeant named Nicholson put the other Marine in a covering position while he attempted to free the war-

3. Marines most often deploy with a Marine Expeditionary Unit (Special Operation Capable), MEU(SOC), on six-month deployments. Numbering more than 2,200 personnel, MEU(SOC)s combine air-combat, ground-combat, and service-support units into one cohesive unit embarked on three Navy vessels. Three MEU(SOC)s are usually at sea: from Camp Lejeune, North Carolina, to the Atlantic and Mediterranean; from Okinawa to the Western Pacific; from Camp Pendleton, California, to the Indian Ocean and Persian Gulf.

rant officer. His legs were trapped under the engine, making it almost impossible for him to be freed by the other two. The sergeant wouldn't leave despite the warrant officer begging for him and the other to save themselves.

"An Army Black Hawk helicopter landed, offering to evacuate the two Marines. They again refused to leave, choosing to remain in danger and protect the Marine in the wreckage. More Army Black Hawks arrived, and the crew of one helped free the pinned Marine as the others provided cover."

"There's a trend, isn't there, Sergeant?" asked Smith.

"And what's the trend?" said Sergeant Lee.

"Marines risking and sacrificing for each other."

"Whether it be the Civil War or today," said Nushi.

"It even expands past us Marines, to soldiers and sailors and airmen working together in the face of extreme adversity," said Sergeant Lee. "Just like those Army helicopter crews coming to help those Marines."

9

Sergeant Timmerman's Tank

If the new American B-29s were to bomb the Japanese mainland, it would be necessary to establish airfields within 1,500 miles of Japan. The Navy also wanted advanced bases so the Japanese Combined Fleet could be drawn out and engaged in a decisive battle. An 800-ship, 162,000-man joint expeditionary force was formed and sent to the Mariana Islands chain. Three islands were selected: Saipan, Tinian, and Guam.

Saipan became the first objective, with a planned D-day of 15 June 1944. It was a tiny island, only fourteen miles long and six wide, but surrounded by coral reefs. Once ashore the invaders would contend with rugged terrain consisting of cliffs, swamps, mountains, and caves, as well as the enemy forces. Saipan was the headquarters of the Japanese Central Pacific Fleet under Admiral Nagumo, previously commander of the Pearl Harbor strike force. United States intelligence estimated there to be well over 30,000 Japanese troops defending the island along with a civilian population of unknown size.

In the first twenty minutes of D-day, 8,000 Marines from the 2d and 4th Marine Divisions went ashore, but they would fight for three days to protect their beachhead. More than 20,000 Americans landed on the first day. With coral reefs limiting the number of accessible beaches, it was not difficult for the Japanese to determine the most likely landing sites. The Marines suffered more than 2,000 casualties in the fierce first day of fighting. The hero of Saipan was the individual rifleman:

Barely out of boyhood, often scared and sometimes blindly heroic, he fought and conquered—and created the image of the modern Marine Corps. On his head rests a helmet covered with camouflage cloth; his light green cotton dungaree with black USMC globe and anchor on the left pocket are stained and often bloody; his M-1 is scratched but clean; his leggings (if he still has them) cover soft brown work shoes; around his waist hangs a cartridge belt carrying two canteens, a first-aid packet, and a Ka-Bar knife.[1]

The bloody battle went on for three and half weeks, costing 3,426 American dead and 13,099 wounded, but enemy dead were estimated at more than 32,800. It ended on 9 July, one day after a savage banzai attack that could only have had the purpose of killing more Americans before the battle ended. After the war one Japanese admiral said, "our war was lost with the loss of Saipan."[2]

"This obstacle is named in honor of Grant F. Timmerman," said Sergeant Lee. It was 1235, the sun was now high in the sky and the heat was beginning to rise. The recruits' uniforms were still damp from the mud on the endurance course, so they felt both sticky and hot. There had been some snacking between obstacles, but in reality they had already missed two full meals. "Timmerman was born in Americus, Kansas, on 19 February 1919, and worked as a welder in California before joining the Marine Corps in 1937. He served for thirty-three straight months in China, earning a letter of commendation for coming to the rescue of a woman surrounded by an angry Chinese mob. He left the Marine Corps in late 1941, only to rejoin shortly after the attack on Pearl Harbor. He fought on

1. Millett, Allan R., *Semper Fidelis: The Story of the United States Marine Corps*, rev. and expanded ed. (New York, Free Press, 1991) 419.
2. Moskin, J. Robert, *The U.S. Marine Corps Story*, 3d ed. (New York, McGraw Hill, 1992) 329. Quoting Shaw Jr., Nalty, Turnblahd, *Central Pacific Drive* (New York, Back Bay Books, 1992) 346 (published simultaneously in Canada by Little, Brown & Company).

Tarawa in November 1943, and landed on D-day for the battle of
Saipan. Timmerman would be an early casualty, wounded in the
right forearm by shrapnel, but he refused to stop. He received
the Bronze Star for valor and kept on fighting, finally earning the
Medal of Honor.

The President of the United States in the name of The Congress
takes pleasure in presenting the Medal of Honor posthumously to
Sergeant Grant F. Timmerman, United States Marine Corps, for service set forth in the following citation:

> For conspicuous gallantry and intrepidity at the risk of his
> life above and beyond the call of duty as tank commander serv-
> ing with the 2d Battalion, 6th Marines, 2d Marine Division,
> during action against enemy Japanese forces on Saipan, Mar-
> ianas Islands, on 8 July 1944. Advancing with his tank a few
> yards ahead of the infantry in support of a vigorous attack on
> hostile positions, Sergeant Timmerman maintained steady
> fire from his antiaircraft sky-mount machine gun until
> progress was impeded by a series of enemy trenches and pill-
> boxes. Observing a target of opportunity, he immediately or-
> dered the tank stopped and, mindful of the danger from the
> muzzle blast as he prepared to open fire with the 75mm, fear-
> lessly stood up in the exposed turret and ordered the infantry
> to hit the deck. Quick to act as a grenade, hurled by the Japan-
> ese, was about to drop into the open turret hatch, Sergeant
> Timmerman unhesitatingly blocked the opening with his
> body, holding the grenade against his chest and taking the
> brunt of the explosion. His exceptional valor and loyalty in sav-
> ing his men at the cost of his own life reflect the highest credit
> upon Sergeant Timmerman and the United States Naval Ser-
> vice. He gallantly gave his life in the service of his country.
> Signed, Harry S. Truman[3]

3. Medal of Honor citation from *The Congressional Medal of Honor, The
Names, The Deeds* (Chico, Calif., Sharp and Dunnigan, 1988) 460.

There was not a lot to this obstacle: Four thick boards, ten feet long and six inches wide. There were three-foot sections of rope attached throughout the length of each board. A footlocker held several gas masks, and there was a path on which it was obvious the boards had traveled.

"Although the other two tank crewmen were slightly wounded, Sergeant Timmerman received all of the large fragments and was killed instantly," said Sergeant Lee.

"Sergeant, Recruit Northwood requests permission to speak," said a man who was completely different from the other recruits. He was twenty-six and had worked at several odd jobs over the past eight years. He barely passed the initial strength test. The physical training was difficult for him, leading to his being at the rear of most runs. His maturity was beneficial to the platoon, but he kept to himself too much to be one of the squad leaders. At twenty-six, sharing a room with some fifty eighteen-year-old men was difficult.

"First of all, you're done with all that hoopla," said Sergeant Lee. "Just stand there and talk to me man to man, just like Marines do. No need to ask permission to speak. Marines don't do that; just be respectful like we taught you."

"I want to be the leader for this one, Sergeant," said Northwood. For some reason, maybe because of his age, Northwood felt a link with Timmerman. Another fact was that Timmerman's picture gave Northwood the feeling that he had something in common with him. Timmerman looked to be a small man, scholarly looking with a pair of wire-framed eyeglasses. Northwood looked the same way, growing up being called a pencil-necked geek most of his life.

Northwood joined to do something different and had no serious regrets. He'd bounced from job to job, even trying to complete a little college, but never got anywhere. Nothing appealed to him, so he found himself nearing thirty still without any real direction in life. One day he just walked into a recruiter's office and signed up, shipping to boot camp within a week.

"Okay, good to go, Northwood," said Sergeant Lee. "You're the leader. The enemy has chemically contaminated an area that you must cross for an attack on an enemy position. The chemical contaminant is not only deadly, but corrosive, and it will eat through the leather of your boots if they come in contact with it. There are several boards with ropes attached nearby." Sergeant Lee pointed to the four boards. "Your mission is to cross the contaminated area and link up with your platoon for the attack. You will wear your load-bearing vest, a gas mask, and sling your rifle over your back, muzzle down.

"Coordinating instructions: One, do not place the wooden rails end to end. Two, if a recruit touches the ground, that recruit is eliminated from the problem. Three, if a rope touches the deck, it can not be used again. Are there any questions?"

"Yes, Sergeant," said Northwood. He was now sorry for volunteering because this obstacle was going to pose some different challenges. "We're going to stand on the boards like one would stand on snow skis, and use the ropes to shuffle across the contaminated area?"

"Well, are you asking me a question or briefing me on your plan?" laughed Sergeant Lee.

"I just want to make sure I understand, Sergeant," said Northwood.

"Oh yeah, you understand, 'cause that's a pretty good plan of attack," said Sergeant Lee.

Northwood conferred with the other recruits for a few seconds, and they all agreed that his plan was sound. It was necessary to split the squad into two groups, with Simms put in charge of the second group. Each group used two boards, with one under all their left feet and the other under all their right. They took the ropes in their hands and used them to lift the boards so they could walk with them. Every step had to be coordinated, for a man who failed to lift his leg with the others would cause the group to falter.

"Left," everyone lifted his left leg and took a small step. "Right," another with the right. "Left . . . right . . . left . . . right . . . left . . ."

Northwood made a key mistake by trying to lead from the front when he should have placed himself in a position where he could best control the unit. It was a common mistake, which some new officers or noncommissioned officers made, ending up walking too closely to the point man of a combat patrol.

Because Northwood was the first on his board, the other recruits could not clearly hear his commands through their gas masks, and there were problems with getting a good rhythm going. He identified this within the first few steps, but could not get off the board and touch the ground without being eliminated.

"Simms," Northwood yelled, voice muffled by the gas mask. Simms's group had not started yet. "Put yourself in the middle so everyone can hear you." Now that he had passed on the lesson of his mistake to the other group, Northwood needed to find a way to make things work better for his group. At first he attempted to turn his head and shout back towards the squad, but that didn't work well either. Finally, realizing that he was too concerned with his being the one giving the commands, Northwood shouted instructions to Mascuzzio who was positioned in the middle. "You're going to have to give the commands, so everyone can hear," he said.

With Mascuzzio giving the commands the group started moving along at a good pace. For the first twenty meters it was almost fun, but then it got old pretty quickly. Every time a recruit was a little faster or slower than the others, he threw the whole group off.

"*IF YOU DO THAT AGAIN, WATERS, I'M GOING TO KNOCK YOU OUT*," screamed Hill in the other group. Waters had failed to step at the right time causing Smith to fall off and be eliminated.

The commotion, of course, caught Sergeant Lee's attention. He was going to step in and correct the recruits for arguing and threatening each other, but he decided to let them continue. This often happened, as a tired and stressed-out group of young men became hostile toward one another. By letting them continue, Sergeant Lee was preparing to make a point that could reduce the chances of similar behavior in the future. Such conduct was bad here, but it might be deadly in combat.

At the halfway point, they had to turn around. Northwood's group decided to do it the hard way. They tried to make a U-turn by making small steps, but soon found themselves shuffling back and forth to get headed back in the same direction they'd come from. Simms's group was forced to wait for Northwood to complete the turn, with some of the group trying to give suggestions to the other. The suggestions were not well received, and the two groups were soon griping back and forth at each other.

"*SHUT UP!*" yelled Sergeant Lee. "You sound like a bunch of school kids. Work together!"

The recruits stopped their arguing, finishing the turn with only Northwood giving instructions to Mascuzzio and Simms, and they to their groups. Simms's group completed the turn the easy way. They just turned themselves around on the boards, facing the other way. The front was now the rear and the rear was the front, heading the team in the opposite direction. Other than the commands of "left" and "right," the obstacle was completed in awkward silence. The recruits knew they had not done well.

"Get over there and sit down," snapped Sergeant Lee when the first group was done. He wasn't really angry at their conduct. He merely wanted to use their mistake as an opportunity for them to learn and become better. "Who taught you how to act like that?" he asked when the second group was done. "This obstacle is named after a Marine who exposed himself to enemy fire to signal his fellow Marines to take cover because he was concerned that firing the main gun of the tank might wound the Marine infantrymen. The frustrations he was having with communication was just like the frustration you had from the gas mask, but in his case people's lives were in jeopardy. What if the same were true here, if lives depended on our ability to work through the frustration? What's your fighting with each other going to accomplish? I know that we drill instructors didn't teach you that arguing is how Marines deal with adversity. Did we?"

"No, Sergeant," the squad said.

"You're tired, you're hungry, and things weren't working well, but you just made it worse by your selfish behavior. What went wrong, Northwood?"

"First, I didn't put myself in a good place to control the group I was with, Sergeant."

"You made up for that, though. It was good thinking by having someone else do it for you. What about the rest of you? What were you doing when Northwood was using his head?"

"When Northwood told me to get in the middle . . ."

"Another good move," said Sergeant Lee, interrupting Simms.

". . . I was able to have an easier time giving instructions, but some weren't listening."

"So what's the answer when someone isn't listening to you?"

"I know now that I shouldn't start poppin' off, Sergeant," said Hill.

"All of you were complaining and griping at each other. I've already told you once today that Marines don't win wars by acting like that, haven't I?"

"*YES, SIR,*" sounded the squad. Sergeant Lee was on a roll and he didn't notice that the recruits called him "sir." After three months, it was difficult for them to change their habits.

"Who can tell me what happened on 23 October 1983?" Sergeant Lee needed to make a point to the squad about the importance of maintaining the proper attitude when facing adversity.

"It's the day the Marine barracks in Beirut was destroyed by Hezbollah-backed terrorists," said Smith.

"Two hundred and forty-one Americans were killed and more than eighty were wounded," said Sergeant Lee. "The commandant at the time, Gen. P. X. Kelley, went to the hospital in Wiesbaden, Germany, to visit the wounded. It was a tough time for the Marines and they needed their commandant. One of the men was a lance corporal named Nashton, who was clinging to life. When he couldn't clearly see the commandant's rank, he reached up to touch the four stars on his collar, frantically trying to speak but couldn't. Finally, after he tried to spell something out on the bedsheet, they gave him a pad of paper so he could give General Kelley his message.

"Here's a man about your age with every reason in the world to be bitter. He can't talk, his buddies are dead, he's badly hurt, and what do you think he wrote?"

The recruits didn't answer.

"He wrote *Semper Fi!*" (The Marine motto, meaning *Always Faithful!*) "With the little life he had left in his body, he wanted his commandant to know that he was still a proud Marine." Sergeant Lee waited for a few seconds before saying anything. "Why could he stay motivated from a hospital bed, but you fall apart during something like this?"

"He was a Marine," said Nushi.

"So? You're as close as one can come to being one. You'll be Marines in less than two days. Why could he do it? How did Timmerman give his life for the other two men in his tank?"

"Because they weren't thinking of themselves," said Waters.

"Outbursts like the one you had on this obstacle tell me you're still being selfish. At the last station you were telling me about Marines working together. You can give me the right answers to the questions, but when push comes to shove and we're talking about action, you fall apart. We've got a long way to go. A long way indeed."

10

Reaction Course

The reaction course was made up of six obstacles, similar to the warrior stations but designed to require more decision making. Each was like a giant puzzle where the recruits had to solve problems to accomplish a mission. They were given several pieces of equipment to use, but usually the equipment was not sufficient for the task. Imagination from the recruits was needed if the squad was to be successful.

The first obstacle had a sawdust pit to represent a deep river, with overhanging pipes that resembled a bridge. The squad was told they had personnel-detection sensors to deliver to another unit. Along the way, they came to the remains of a destroyed bridge, and now needed to find a way to the far side within fifteen minutes. All the men and gear had to cross the river. To aid their movement the squad had several planks, a rope, two fifty-five-gallon drums, and a can representing the sensors. The barrels could "float" in the sawdust pit, but positive control had to be maintained or they would float away. If a man or any other piece of gear touched the "water," it would be eliminated from the problem.

The squad wasted no time, immediately building a bridge by using the barrels as pontoons. Construction progressed quickly, but when half complete it was obvious that they did not have enough planks. They made a common recruit mistake: failing to analyze the individual tasks needed to accomplish the mission. The squad went straight from "A" to "D," not recognizing the need to go through "B" and "C."

The bridge was dismantled and the recruits began again, thus wasting valuable time. On their second attempt the squad rotated

103

the placement of the planks. They built enough of a bridge to get a few recruits to the pipes, and then used the same material to build another bridge to the opposite side of the obstacle. Unfortunately, they wasted too much time in the beginning to complete their mission. They failed.

Sergeant Lee used the debrief as an opportunity to discuss what the squad could do to improve their problem solving, avoiding his opinion of the "right" way to accomplish the mission. The recruits would never again find themselves in this exact situation. Lee needed to help them learn how to think and solve problems, not how to build a bridge out of planks and fifty-five-gallon barrels.

On the second obstacle the squad was told that they were carrying vital supplies to their platoon, located across a river. They came to another destroyed bridge, but some portions still remained. Some of the remaining parts were booby trapped, and the squad was told to be alert for enemy in the area. Several posts protruded from another sawdust pit, some painted red to represent that they were booby trapped. The squad was given three planks of various sizes, with the mission to get all recruits and equipment across.

This time the squad thought before they acted, not making the mistake of their first reaction-course station. After a long debate about the best way to accomplish the mission, the squad finally began. When the fifteen-minute time limit was reached, the squad was still only halfway across because of the time they took talking about their plan. They failed again.

At the third station the squad was to deliver explosives to an engineer platoon. While en route, they ran into a large minefield that could not be avoided. There was a wall in the center of the minefield, which created a way to cross safely. Enemy patrols were in the area and checked the minefield every twenty minutes, so they needed to hurry to avoid any loud noise that might alert the enemy. The men were given a twelve-foot ladder, a box representing the explosives, and a twelve-foot rope. If a team member or piece of gear touched the ground or any red area, it would be eliminated from the problem. For security reasons, they had to take everything, including the ladder. All team members had to cross over the obstacle.

The squad quickly came up with a plan and began to execute it. They tied the rope to one end of the ladder and carefully lowered it against the wall in the middle of the minefield, cautious not to make any loud noise. It now leaned against the fence at a thirty-degree angle from the ground. The squad walked on the ladder across the minefield and then climbed up over the wall, bringing the box of explosives with them. The last man tied the rope to the opposite end of the ladder so it could be lifted across once everyone was past the minefield. They passed.

For station number four the squad was told that they were just attacked by a small enemy force. They repelled the attack, but the enemy might return at any time. One team member was wounded from the firefight and was lying on the other side of a storm drain. Their mission was to go through the storm drain and over several holes to retrieve the injured Marine and bring him to the other side for medical evacuation by helicopter. The only gear they received was a plank and a stretcher.

The recruits used the plank to traverse the gaps of the obstacle, leapfrogging toward the dummy representing an injured Marine. Because there was only one plank, it was necessary to pass it back and forth. Little by little the squad moved men through the storm drain. When they had sufficient men to lift the dummy, they placed him on the stretcher and reversed the process with the plank, returning to the starting point. They made it to the helicopter landing site before the time limit, thus accomplishing the mission.

On station number five the recruits were to deliver ammunition to a platoon in a city. They were to use the city's sewer system to avoid enemy detection, but, along the way they found that an artillery barrage had destroyed part of the sewer. The platoon was in desperate need of ammunition, so they had to find a way through the destroyed portion quickly. They were given two planks and a rope, as well as several cans representing the ammunition. All team members had to make it across the obstacle.

The squad used the planks to position men at key points across the obstacle. They then passed the rope across, making sure that the end at the far side was lower than the end at the near side. The ammunition cans were moved down the rope one at a time, with the recruits following on the planks. After the mission was accomplished, the recruits lost two men trying to bring all the planks with them. Sergeant Lee pointed out during the debrief that bringing all the gear was not a requirement on this station. They could have thrown the planks into the sewer once done with them. They accomplished the mission, but lost two men because they didn't listen to the instructions or ask any questions to clarify the mission.

At the last reaction-course station the recruits faced another river with a washed-out bridge. Their mission was to cross the river and deliver important communication gear. They were issued two eight-foot pipes, a rope, and one large ammunition can representing the communication gear. All team members and gear had to make it across.

The squad leaned the pipes against the remains of the bridge and shimmied up. Once they got a few men on the bridge, they sent two all the way to the other side. Pulling the communication gear up the pipes proved to be challenging. It kept twisting, requiring the recruits to move the pipes several times to prevent the gear from falling into the "water." Once the communication gear made it to the other side, the remaining recruits followed. Utilizing teamwork and good communication, they successfully accomplished the mission.

The squad accomplished four of the six missions, taking a few "casualties" in the process. Their success rate wasn't as important as Lee seeing that the recruits had learned something from their mistakes. Because they'd been awake for fifteen hours, hiked almost twelve miles, and were about to miss a third meal, making decisions did not come easily. The body fatigue affected the mind's ability to function properly, causing the recruits to be put in situations that could make simple problems difficult to solve. That was good, because little was learned when everything went perfectly.

Failure could be used to identify weaknesses to be strengthened, reducing future mistakes. It's not easy to instill the desire to do what was the harder right, rather than take an easy shortcut. Sergeant Lee wanted to produce a Marine who, when given the proverbial command to "jump," wouldn't even bother asking how high, but instantly jumped as high as he could; individuals who do their best, regardless of how trivial the task, and that always look out for the group before themselves. This kind of initiative needs to be combined with judgment to prevent it from being counterproductive or even destructive.

Developing the recruits' problem-solving skills was important, because Marines need to be capable of making decisions for the Corps' doctrine of maneuver warfare to be successful. Maneuver warfare is dependent on military judgment at all levels, as all Marines become capable of making decisions that lead to the unit's accomplishing its mission. A military decision does not have a mathematical answer. It requires both intuitive skill to recognize and analyze, and creative ability to devise a practical solution. The reaction course helped break through the last vestiges of the "you-don't-get-paid-to-think" mentality in Marine Corps recruit training. Failure to make good decisions not only has the potential for tragic consequences on the battlefield, but also for a Marine on liberty in the civilian world.

Considering the challenges of the modern world, it is clear that what may have been successful in the past may not be successful now or in the future. To survive, and more so to thrive, Marines must not only possess discipline and the ability to work together, but also the ability to solve problems and distinguish between right and wrong. Training needs to be tough, include core values, require problem solving, and utilize teamwork. In other words, it needs to be just like the Crucible.

11

Sergeant Cukela's Wall

In the summer of 1914, Germany invaded Belgium and swept through the country toward Paris. The French were able to stop them in the Battle of the Marne, where nineteenth-century tactics met with twentieth-century weapons to create a standstill that led to brutal trench warfare for the next four years, bloody and costly for both sides. On 6 April 1917, the United States entered the war, five months after President Wilson was reelected using a HE KEPT US OUT OF THE WAR campaign slogan.

The Marine Corps prepared for war by increasing their recruiting effort and calling the new Marine Corps Reserve (consisting of three officers and thirty-three enlisted) to active duty. A Marine brigade was part of the first convoy of ships headed to Europe, but they would have to wait for combat. General John Pershing tasked them with such mundane duties as line-of-communication troops and military police. Marines were thought to be useful only in small detachments aboard ships and naval stations, not as a conventional land army.

In early 1918, Marine forces finally were brought together to form a brigade commanded by Brig. Gen. Charles Doyen, numbering more than 9,000 men. The overall situation was grim after great German success in the Third Battle of the Aisne, so the American 2d Infantry Division, of which the Marine 4th Brigade was an intregal part, was sent to help the French XXI Corps contain the Germans at the Marne River near Château-Thierry. The Marines were sent to a quiet portion of the defenses southeast of Verdun where they saw little action at first.

When the Germans attacked in May with more than forty divisions, a French officer is rumored to have suggested to the Marines that it was time to retreat. "Retreat? Hell! We just got here," was the Marine response. There was debate over who actually made the statement, but it clearly summarized the Marine mood.

In early June, the Marines were formed near a German strong point in the Bois de Belleau, or Belleau Wood. From the Marines' position they could see a sea of wheat, rolling in the hot wind, with the wood sitting a half-mile away. The battle began with exchanges of artillery fire, and then German infantrymen appeared, approaching rapidly. The Marine Corps had faced many foes through its 143 year history, but probably none as frightening as the battle-hardened German soldier. The brigade opened up with their Springfield rifles at 800 yards, pushing the Germans back to the shelter of the Wood. Marines stopped more attempts to cross the wheat field, but the tables would soon reverse.

On 6 June, Marines went "over the top," attacking from their trenches toward the Wood. The attack faltered at first, with relentless machine-gun fire ripping Marine units apart. The advance continued on hands and knees, occasionally with a rush covered by gunfire. Finally, GSgt. Dan Daily (recipient of two Medals of Honor for action in Peking and Haiti, and soon to be awarded the Navy Cross) swung his bayoneted rifle and yelled, "Come on you sons of bitches, do you want to live forever?" The survivors of the wheat field surged forward, overrunning the first German line to gain a toehold.

For the next nineteen days, the fighting in the woods was bitter and brutal. In clouds of deadly mustard gas and armed with their Springfields and bayonets, the Marines fought hand-to-hand with the Germans. When a private's gas mask was shot from his face, a veteran gunnery sergeant gave his mask to the young Marine. The gunny saved the private's life by sacrificing his own. Raw courage like that carried the Marines forward.

Attack and counterattack, positions in the tangle of shattered trees and dead bodies changed hands. The Germans were slowly overwhelmed by the tenacious fighting, referring to the Marines as *Teufelhunden*—Devil Dogs. The official German report would further comment, calling Marines vigorous, self-confident, and remarkable marksmen. They would also assign their highest rating of "storm trooper" to the Marine units.[1] Finally, on 26 June, the 5th Marines wiped out the last German strong point and sent a message: "Woods now U.S. Marine Corps entirely."[2] The price was horrific: 126 officers and 5,057 enlisted men were dead or wounded, more than half of the Marine brigade.

The French people recognized the fabulous Marine performance with cheers of "Vive les Marines" when the Marine Corps flag was seen in the streets of Paris, and a French general ordered that henceforth Belleau Wood be called *"Bois de la Brigade de Marine."* A young assistant secretary of the Navy named Franklin D. Roosevelt would tour the Wood a few weeks later, authorizing enlisted Marines to wear the Marine Emblem on their uniform collars to recognize their splendid work. Until then, wearing the emblem on the collar was considered an officer's privilege.

The Germans weren't beaten yet, but the balance of power was beginning to shift. The Germans were losing men and fighting power, while the Allies had fresh Americans joining their ranks regularly. On 15 July, forty-nine German divisions again lunged toward Paris, crossing the Marne for a short time but, then, finally thrown back with heavy casualties on both sides of the lines. The Allies decided to counterattack near Soissons with the Marines leading the initial assault. On the night of 17 July, they moved through the mud and rain to their attack positions in the Forest of Retz. At 0435, 18 July, the 5th Marines led on the 2d Division line, advancing more than two miles after which the 6th Marines passed through and went another mile and a half before reaching the division objective on 19 July. Once again, the fighting was brutal and costly. One company commander sent a scribbled message to higher headquarters, ". . . I have only two men left out of my company and twenty out of other

---

1. German report: "The Second American Division must be considered a very good one and may even perhaps be reckoned as a storm troop. The different attacks at Belleau Wood were carried out with bravery and dash."
2. Alexander, Joseph H., *A Fellowship of Valor: The Battle History of the United States Marines* (New York, HarperCollins, 1997) 41.

companies . . . I have no one on my left, and only a few on my right. I will hold."[3] Not only did the Marines hold, they moved forward!

Marines would fight 12–16 September at Saint-Mihiel, where history was made when Major General Lejeune was named by General Pershing to command the 2d Infantry Division. He was the first and only Marine general to command an Army division. Fighting moved on to Blanc Mont Ridge on 2–9 October, a position the Germans had been fortifying since 1914. The final fighting along the Argonne Forest and Muese River, 1–11 November, proved especially brutal.

By war's end at 1100, 11 November 1918, more than 38,000 Marines had served in Europe and the Corps established itself as a viable fighting force on the modern battlefield. Marine victories helped the commandant breathe new life into plans to expand the Corps. Congress approved a wartime strength of 3,017 officers and 75,500 men, compared to 341 officers and 10,056 men in 1916. The price of success was high however, with 2,457 dead and 8,894 wounded. Eight were awarded the Medal of Honor.

The 5th and 6th Regiments received the French fourragère, an award that present members of those units continue to wear today. The Marines' contribution helped turn the tide of the war, as the German chancellor said of the battle at Soissons, "The history of the world played out in three days."[4]

"This obstacle is named in honor of Louis Cukela," said Sergeant Lee. It was now 1640, the hot afternoon was beginning to cool and the Crucible only had a little more than thirty-nine hours remaining. "He was born in Serbia in 1888 and emigrated to the United States in 1913. In 1914, he enlisted in the Army and was discharged in 1916. In 1917, with World War I raging, Cukela enlisted in the Marine Corps and was sent to France. Because of his Army experience, he quickly rose to the rank of sergeant."

3. Simmons, Edwin, *The United States Marine Corps: 1775—1975* (New York, Viking Press, 1976) 114.
4. Moskin, J. Robert, *The U.S. Marine Corps Story*, 3d ed. (New York, McGraw Hill, 1992) 329. Quoting Harbord, James G., *The American Army in France: 1917–1919* (Boston, Little, Brown & Company, 1918) 337.

The obstacle was a wall, fifteen feet high and ten feet wide. Constructed of flat wood planks, there was nothing that could be used to help assist the recruits in getting over it. There was a small platform on the opposite side, where a man could stand if he could get himself to the top.

Citation: For extraordinary heroism while serving with the 66th Company, 5th Regiment, during action in the Forest de Retz, near Villers-Cotterêts, France, 18 July 1918. Sergeant Cukela advanced alone against an enemy strong point that was holding up his line. Disregarding the warnings of his comrades, he crawled out from the flank in the face of heavy fire and worked his way to the rear of the enemy position. Rushing a machine-gun emplacement, he killed or drove off the crew with his bayonet, bombed out the remaining part of the strong point with German handgrenades and captured two machine guns and four men.[5]

As with Corporal Mackie's citation, the recruits noticed that the citation was not as descriptive as some others. Sergeant Lee told the recruits how Sergeant Cukela fought in the battle at Forest de Retz south of Soissons that was referred to as "two days in hell" due to the July heat. His heroic actions as written in the citation led to the Marines' breaking through the German defenses. The Marine Brigade lost 2,015 men killed and wounded, but the battle triggered the general retreat of the German Army. Sergeant Cukela's actions were so significant that he received the Medal of Honor from both the Navy and the Army, the Medaille Militaire from France, Croce al Merito di Guerra from Italy, and the Commander's Cross of the Royal Order of the Crown of Yugoslavia. He also received a field appointment to the rank of second lieutenant in September 1918, and later retired as a major in June of 1940. During World War II he was recalled to active duty and retired, for a second time, in May of 1946 with more than

5. Medal of Honor citation from *The Congressional Medal of Honor, The Names, The Deeds* (Chico, Calif., Sharp and Dunnigan, 1988) 512.

thirty-two years of active service. On 19 March 1956, he died and was buried with full military honors at Arlington National Cemetery.

"Any volunteers for this one?" asked Sergeant Lee.

"I'll do it, Sergeant," said Recruit Nol, who came to the United States with his parents from Cambodia when he was fourteen years old. He still, unfortunately, was learning the language. He had lived in Los Angeles during the past four years, and missed his parents terribly. The family had gone through a lot together, and the parents still barely spoke English. They therefore relied on Nol for many things. His leaving for boot camp was a complete shock to them, so during the first few weeks the senior drill instructor and lieutenant had to help him find assistance for the family.

Nol enlisted from a strong sense of indebtedness to America; joining the Corps seemed the most American thing he could do. His language problem made things difficult for the drill instructor team. They initially were concerned that he would fail his academic evaluations, but with a little extra attention he did well.

"Okay, Nol, you're the squad leader," said Sergeant Lee. "Your platoon is pinned down by enemy fire from a bunker. Your squad was moving around the bunker to attack it from the rear when you ran into a large wall." Sergeant Lee pointed to the wall behind him. The small platform allowed some of the recruits to stand on the top of the wall, but first they would have to scale it from the open side.

"Your mission is to get over the wall to attack the enemy bunker on the other side. You will wear your helmets, flak jackets, and load-bearing vests. You'll pass your rifles over the obstacle.

"Coordinating instructions: One, do *not* lift a man by his load-bearing vest. Two, recruits will be positioned in the front and back of the wall to catch anyone who falls. Three, once a team member goes over the wall and comes down the opposite side, he may serve as a spotter, but he may not assist others in getting over the wall. Four, do not use the rope connected on the rear of the wall to scale the front of the wall." The rope was there to aid the men in getting down the other side. "Five, do not jump off the wall on either side. Are there any questions?"

"Yes, Sergeant," said Nol. "Once we get someone on top, can they help the others?"

"Yes, of course. As long as they are still on top, they can help pull others up. If they're on the ground they can only be spotters positioned for safety to catch someone who falls."

Nol surprised Sergeant Lee by how well he took charge and began to organize the squad. He'd been rather quiet before, but one could expect leadership ability considering the amount of responsibility he accepted on the part of his family. He gave specific instructions on how he wanted a human pyramid built to allow others to climb up to the top of the wall. He sent two of the huskier recruits up first, because their upper body strength would be needed to pull others up. The heavier men went next, with the short ones following behind.

The recruits were obviously tired, so it was becoming evident that even the strong could not perform simple tasks without assistance. Muscles ached from the constant strain, and the lack of proper nutrition magnified the pain and prevented rejuvenation. The last two recruits on the ground were Simms and Hill, the two tallest. Hill boosted Simms up to where the others could grab his arms and pull him up. Finally, Hill was lifted up by hanging Simms over the side of the wall. At first the other recruits held Simms's legs, but the discomfort of being held upside down was too much for him. They tried again, holding him by the arms with his armpits on the wall's top. Hill climbed up his back as if Simms were a human ladder. It was painful for Simms, but worked for the team.

After fifteen hours of continuous teamwork, the squad knew who was best at what. Some were thinkers, a couple were pullers, others were lifters, and a few were just good team players. The obstacles would become easier and easier unless they began to argue with one another again. They already learned how to systematically analyze problems and come up with solutions.

"Why was that so easy, Nol?" asked Sergeant Lee.

"Because many of these obstacles are similar. There is always something that we need to get over, under, or through."

"We're working better as a team, too, Sergeant," said Simms.

"So the course isn't challenging anymore?"

"No, Sergeant," said Nol. "It's still real hard."

"As we work together better, things become easier, Sergeant," said Smith.

"The teamwork is what makes things seem easy," said Nushi.

"Is teamwork easy?" asked Sergeant Lee. He called on Waters who was shaking his head, "Why isn't it easy?"

"It's not that it's hard," said Waters, "it's more that it's easy to get tired of each other."

The other recruits laughed and some nodded in agreement.

"Sometimes it's just easier to be an individual," said one of the recruits.

"Sergeant Cukela acted as an individual though, right?" asked Sergeant Lee. "He advanced alone."

"Yes, Sergeant," said Hill, "but he was gaining a toehold. Kind of the same way it was easier on the rest of our squad when we got someone on top of the wall to pull others up, Sergeant Cukela got in a position that made things easier on his fellow Marines."

"So did he use teamwork?" asked Sergeant Lee.

"Yes, Sergeant," said the squad.

"How?"

"He supported the team with his actions," said Mascuzzio.

"What do you think inspired Sergeant Cukela to advance alone against an enemy strong point?" asked Sergeant Lee.

"Courage," said Nol. "Courage and commitment to his fellow Marines."

"Marines just do that type of stuff," said Sergeant Lee. "On the second day of the ground war in Kuwait a young Private First Class named Hren earned a Bronze Star for heroism. A young man, much like all of you. Finding himself face to face with soldiers of an enemy mechanized brigade, he and other Marines bravely fought the armored vehicles on foot. There was a dense fog that made visibility next to nothing, and when an Iraqi vehicle disappeared into the fog, Hren went running into the fog after it.

"Being fired at by machine guns from the vehicle, Hren jumped into an abandoned trench line and began to fire his squad automatic weapon at the enemy. He was able to suppress the Iraqi fire enough for another Marine to get a shot off from an AT4 antitank missile, disabling the vehicle. Then the Iraqis got out and tried to continue the fight, but Hren killed them before they could do any damage to the Marines.

"How were Private first class Hren and Sergeant Cukela able to be so courageous?" asked Sergeant Lee.

"Probably in much the same way we've been trained," said Smith, "that courage isn't the absence of fear, but the ability to overcome it."

"Part of it is understanding that fear is a natural response," said Sergeant Lee. "If you don't think you're going to have to deal with it, you're setting yourself up for failure. Sergeant Cukela was probably afraid when he advanced alone against the Germans, but his courage helped turn the tide of the battle."

"Both Cukela and Hren put their fellow Marines before their own safety," said Simms.

"They both did things that supported other team members," said Smith.

"And remember, Sergeant Cukela only came to this country a few years before the war," said Sergeant Lee. "He was born in Serbia and immigrated here, and immigration is part of America too. Some families came here generations ago, while others, like you, Nol, just did it recently. How many of you are descended from someone who immigrated to the United States?"

Each of the recruits raised his hand.

12

Private First Class Anderson's Fall

According to surviving rosters, at least three African Americans served in the Continental Marines. The first was John Martin whose service began in April of 1777. African Americans again started to serve in the Corps in 1942 when President Roosevelt established the Fair Employment Practices Commission. Most were volunteers, with only a few selected draftees being sent to boot camp in 1943. Among the recruits were college graduates and veterans of other services. Because the country was still segregated, they were trained at Monford Point, North Carolina. The new recruits said they had tough but fair treatment from their white drill instructors. Later, eight black drill instructors were named: Charles Allen, Arnold Bostic, Thomas Brokaw, Mortiner Cox, Edgar Davis, Edgar Huff, George Jackson, and Gilbert "Hashmark" Johnson (Monford Point is now named Camp Johnson).

Regardless of the uniform, racial discrimination was common. Black Marines still had to ride in the back of the bus and much of Jacksonville, North Carolina, shut its doors when they first entered town on liberty. Marine Corps officials provided trucks to carry the black Marines to towns with large black populations so they could enjoy their time off.

The last white drill instructors left Monford Point in May 1942. Training was still supervised by white officers, because there were no black officers until the latter part of World War II. On 10 November 1945, Frederick Branch became the first black commissioned officer. This was two years before Jackie Robinson would become the first black in Major League baseball and several decades before the civil rights movement began. Branch battled through the racism and ignorance of the times, unable to eat at the same restaurants as his white peers or subordinates. Today, a building at the Corps' Officer Candidate School in Quantico, Virginia, is named Branch Hall in honor of this pioneer.

During World War II, black Marines served primarily in ammunition and depot companies, which provided working parties for various labor details. They were segregated units not specifically intended to fight in combat, but they still participated in several campaigns. Their first such experience came on Saipan, where Pfc. Kenneth Tibbs was the first black Marine to die in combat. The 3d Ammunition Company received the Presidential Unit Citation for their role on Saipan, and the 6th Ammunition Company was awarded the Navy Unit Commendation on Iwo Jima. Black Marines also served in the battle for Okinawa and during occupation duty in Japan. The highest personal decoration was the Silver Star earned by Pfc. Luther Woodward on Guam.

President Truman ordered an end to segregation in 1949, closing Monford Point and sending all recruits to San Diego or Parris Island. Shortly thereafter, Annie Graham became the first black female to enlist in the Corps on 8 September 1949. Recruit training was desegregated and the Corps fought for the first time with integrated units during the Korean War. Master Sergeant Edgar Huff was the company gunnery sergeant and the only black in Weapons Company, 2d Battalion, 1st Marines. He later served as the company first sergeant. "Hashmark" Johnson served in the billets of first sergeant, sergeant major, and advisor to Korean forces and stated, "I didn't encounter any difficulty. I accepted each individual for what he was and apparently they accepted me for what I was."[1]

Private first class A. C. Clark distinguished himself by earning the Bronze Star in August 1952 and the Silver Star a few months later in December. In the first action, he rescued his platoon leader who'd been wounded. In the second, he ignored his own wounds to cover the evacuation of two wounded Marines. Lieutenant William Jenkins became the first black Marine to lead Marines into combat in

1. Donnelly, R. W. and H. I. Shaw, *Blacks in the Marine Corps* (Washington, D.C., HQMC) 58.

Company B, 1st Battalion, 7th Marines. Lieutenant Frank Peterson was the first black pilot. He flew sixty-four combat missions and received the Distinguished Flying Cross.

By the Vietnam War, the Corps was fully integrated, and of the 448,000 Marines who served in-country more than 41,000 were black. There is no way to calculate the number of awards for heroism, but five earned the Medal of Honor. The senior black officer was now Lt. Col. Frank Peterson, who commanded a phantom-jet attack squadron in Chu Lai. He was the first African American to command a tactical air squadron in either the Navy or the Marine Corps. He was shot down, rescued, and received the Legion of Merit during his tour in Vietnam. Peterson would later be promoted to major general, the Corps' first African-American Marine to wear stars.

In May 1968, Monford Point graduate (April 1943) Sgt. Maj. Agrippa Smith went to the White House to accept the Presidential Unit Citation on behalf of the enlisted Marines from the 26th Marine Regiment for their performance during the siege of Khe Sanh. In 1969, Lt. Col. Hurdle Maxwell took over 1st Battalion, 6th Marines to become the first black Marine to command an infantry battalion. Sergeant Major Edgar R. Huff became the first black sergeant major of an infantry battalion and later he was the senior sergeant major in the Corps. He served two tours in Vietnam and was severely wounded while rescuing a radioman trapped in an open field by enemy fire. In 1972, he retired as the first black Marine with thirty years of service.

Charles Bolden, a black Marine pilot with more than one hundred combat missions in Vietnam, was selected as an astronaut candidate in 1980. He participated in his first space-shuttle mission on the *Columbia* in 1986 and piloted the *Discovery* in 1990. In 1992, he commanded a mission on the space shuttle *Atlantis,* and in 1994, did the same on the *Discovery,* the first joint U.S. and Russian space mission. By the time the 1968 Naval Academy graduate and future Marine general was done with his four missions, he had more than 680 hours in space.

The members of 4th squad were good examples of the diversity of the Corps. Three were African American, two Hispanic, six Caucasian, two Asian Pacific, one Native American.

Asian-Pacific Americans[2] served in the United States military as far back as the Spanish-American War, with nine earning the Medal of Honor. World War II was the turning point though and Asian-Pacific Americans served as a vital part of the American war effort. Chinese Americans followed the lead of their homeland (China declared war on Japan the day after Pearl Harbor) to fight the Japanese. Thousands of Filipinos fought beside Americans at the Bataan Peninsula. Koreans were invaluable, because some knew the Japanese language and often served as translators. Although their families were placed in "relocation camps," Japanese Americans joined the services and defended their country. They are best known as members of the 442d Regimental Combat Team, which fought in Italy and France, and it was the most heavily decorated such unit in the war. Many fought in the Pacific, but there was little publicity about them. One of their greatest contributions was during the Battle of Midway, where they translated intercepted messages and provided valuable intelligence to American commanders.

Hispanic Americans served with distinction and honor in the armed forces for centuries. During the Revolutionary War they pinned down a large British force at Pensacola, preventing it from joining the Battle of Yorktown. Thirty-eight have earned the Medal of Honor, the highest per-capita rate for any population group in the country. The first Hispanic-American Marine to receive the Medal of Honor was Pvt. France Silva during the Boxer Rebellion in China in 1900. Just by looking at the surnames of the Marines whom the warrior stations were named after is a clear indication of the dedication of Hispanic-American Marines. In every war, on every battlefield, they have fought to preserve freedom.

Native Americans have served in the United States military since the early 1800s and twenty have been awarded the Medal of Honor. Iwo Jima was the location of one of the most recognized and inspiring war photographs—the flag raising on Mount Suribachi. One

2. The term "Asian-Pacific American" is used to identify individuals from at least twenty-nine different countries. These persons each have their own unique culture and contribution to the United States.

of the six who took part in the flag raising was Ira Hayes, a Native American from Bapchule, Arizona. Hayes was Pima Indian and raised on the Gila River Indian Reservation. Native Americans from the Navajo tribe also served as "codetalkers" during World War II.[3] Trained as battlefield radiomen, they spoke in their native language, conversing without fear that the Japanese could break their code. They could encode, transmit, and decode a three-line message in twenty seconds. The codetalkers participated in every assault from 1942 to 1945, serving in all six Marine divisions and the Raider and Parachute Battalions.

"The obstacle that your team is about to complete is named for Pfc. James Anderson Jr. of Compton, California," said Sergeant Lee. "Anderson was born in Los Angeles, California, on 22 January 1947, and enlisted in the Marine Corps in February 1966. He arrived in Vietnam in December 1966 and was the first African-American Marine to receive the Medal of Honor."

The time was 1720 hours, the recruits' uniforms were filthy and caked with mud from their day of challenges. Their muscles felt empty. The temperature continued to drop, but it was refreshing and not uncomfortable. The Crucible was more than fifteen hours old and there were fewer than thirty-nine hours remaining. At this point, they'd missed three meals, hiked more than thirteen miles, and been on their feet for more than fifteen hours.

The President of the United States in the name of The Congress takes pleasure in presenting the Medal of Honor posthumously to Private First Class James Anderson Jr., United States Marine Corps, for service set forth in the following citation:

For conspicuous gallantry and intrepidity at the risk of his life above and beyond the call of duty [as a rifleman], 2d Platoon, Company F, 2d Battalion, 3d Marines, 3d Marine Division, in Vietnam on 28 February 1967. Company F was advancing in dense jungle northwest of Cam Lo in an effort to extract a heav-

3. Navajo is an unwritten language of extreme complexity.

ily besieged reconnaissance patrol. Private first class Anderson's platoon was the lead element and had advanced only about 200 meters when they were brought under extremely intense enemy small-arms and automatic-weapons fire. The platoon reacted swiftly, getting on line as best they could in the thick terrain, and began returning fire. Private first class Anderson found himself tightly bunched together with the other members of the platoon only twenty meters from the enemy positions. As the firefight continued several of the men were wounded by the deadly enemy assault. Suddenly, an enemy grenade landed in the midst of the Marines and rolled alongside Private first class Anderson's head. Unhesitatingly and with complete disregard for his own personal safety, he reached out, grasped the grenade, pulled it to his chest and curled around it as it went off. Although several Marines received shrapnel from the grenade, his body absorbed the major force of the explosion. In this singularly heroic act, Private first class Anderson saved his comrades from serious injury and possible death. His personal heroism, extraordinary valor, and inspirational supreme self-sacrifice reflected great credit upon himself and the Marine Corps and upheld the highest traditions of the United States Naval Service. He gallantly gave his life for his country. Signed, Lyndon B. Johnson[4]

"Anderson's act was so deliberate that he actually grabbed the grenade and pulled it into him," said Sergeant Lee. "Did you get that part of it?"

"Yes, Sergeant."

"Who wants to be the leader for this one?"

"I will," said Lacy, raising his hand.

"Okay, listen up."

Lacy would have been considered a great kid in any other place, but he was having serious problems with being a Marine recruit. He

4. Medal of Honor citation from *The Congressional Medal of Honor, The Names, The Deeds* (Chico, Calif., Sharp and Dunnigan, 1988) 19.

was a baseball star and student-body officer in high school, but that meant nothing here. He was the type who was always good at things, probably never failed, but, at the same time, may have never challenged himself. He joined more to upset his parents than anything else. His high-and-mighty attitude took a nose dive the first day of training, when he suddenly experienced challenges and some adversity—he was ready to pack up and go home. He first told the senior drill instructor that it was his constitutional right to quit, and then offered to pay $25,000 if he sent him home. The drill instructors still laugh among themselves at that stunt.

"While attempting to clear a building of enemy resistance, one member of your squad has become trapped on the second deck. The building is on fire and the trapped recruit has to jump to safety. Your mission is to catch your buddy as he escapes from the burning building. You will not wear any gear."

Before the squad was a large table that was about four feet by four feet and five feet high. Most already figured out what they were going to do. Much like Garcia's leap, they would jump into the arms of their squad members.

"Coordinating instructions: One, fallers will stand on the platform facing away from the catchers." Sergeant Lee paused and looked around the squad.

"Did you say face away, Sergeant?" asked Lacy.

"That's right," Sergeant Lee grinned, as he gave them a new challenge to face. They would fall backward without seeing where they were going, needing to trust their teammates completely. "You will place your heels on the edge of the platform, cross your arms in front of your chest, and fall with your body straight, held rigid, and with a slightly arched back. Don't bend forward at the waist or sit down. Are there any questions?"

"Are you going to go first, Sergeant?" asked Lacy.

"Of course," answered Sergeant Lee. This obstacle was one about which many Marines joked, calling it the "ice-tea plunge," but few joked when it came to the actual execution. This was a good challenge, and even those who had no fear of heights admitted to some apprehension at falling backward.

Sergeant Lee stood on the table and faced away from the recruits, crossing his arms over his chest so he didn't hit any of them during his fall. With the table being more than five feet high, and the recruits' arms positioned at about four feet high, there was a point where a man wondered if he would be caught before hitting the ground. Speed picked up at the forty-five-degree angle, and it wasn't until Sergeant Lee passed ninety degrees that he was caught.

The other recruits followed their drill instructor's example on the obstacle. Being like him was more important than any fear they might have had of falling. There was little for Lacy to do, other than make sure the squad was ready to catch someone before he fell, and all completed the obstacle with ease. A few of the recruits failed to remain rigid, bending at the waist and hitting their comrades' arms butt first. Those who did not do well tried again immediately, and all passed on the second attempt.

"That's a good job, fourth squad," said Sergeant Lee. "Lots of times recruits start sweating up there. What were you feeling as you stood ready to blindly fall from the platform?"

"I wasn't scared at all, Sergeant," said Waters. "I knew they would catch me."

"Not worried at all, huh?" said Sergeant Lee, rejoicing in Waters's self-confidence, a new side of him. "Was anyone worried about being dropped?" The recruits shook their heads. "I have to admit I was a little concerned," joked Lee. "Falling backward like that just doesn't seem right. Think about what it felt like when you were halfway. What do you imagine Private first class Anderson felt as he pulled the grenade to his chest?"

"He had to be scared," said Simms, "knowing he was going to die."

"Definitely committed to the team," said Hill.

"Not at all to the same level of sacrifice as Anderson's, but the same commitment that Waters says he felt in the rest of you," said Sergeant Lee.

"Did you say he was the first African-American Marine to receive the Medal of Honor, Sergeant?" asked Simms.

"That's right, but remember, there isn't any color among Marines because we're all green. Before, all of you were different, but soon all of us will share a common identity and a common bond—that of a United States Marine."

"So there isn't any racism in the Marine Corps, Sergeant?" asked Simms.

"Of course there is, because the Corps is a people organization. We draw our members from American society, so the occasional problem person is bound to turn up, an ignorant individual who judges others based on stereotypes. Fortunately for us, they are rare. Besides, someone who thinks that way isn't going to make it far in the Corps. How could anyone make it in an outfit as diverse as us? Just look around and see how many different combinations of race there are in our little group. Our diversity is our strength; I saw that for myself in the streets of Los Angeles during the 1992 riots."

"Marines went to the riots?" asked Mascuzzio.

"You're not going to read about it much in any books, but I spent three days and nights helping keep the peace in Anderson's hometown of Compton." Sergeant Lee turned around to look at Private first class Anderson's picture in front of the obstacle.

When the police officers who beat Rodney King were found not guilty at their trial in April 1992, the city of Los Angeles exploded into the most devastating and violent riot in American history. The police were quickly overwhelmed, and then the National Guard, too. By 29 April, fifty-nine people were dead and there was more than $717 million in damages.

After three days of rioting the authorities had limited success reinstating order. They would gain control of the streets during hours of darkness because of the curfew imposed on the city, but when the sun came up the people came back out, and the authorities lost control again. There was so much looting and violence that there seemed to be little hope of pacification. Rioting began to crop up in other cities, even other countries. Finally, with no hope of order within sight, President Bush sent some 1,400 United States Marines from Camp Pendleton to Los Angeles.

The commander of the majority of Marine forces serving in the streets of Los Angeles was Col. Clifford Stanley, an African American and the regimental commander of the 1st Marine Regiment. He was a former staff member of the Naval Academy, a White House Fellow, and a future Marine Corps general.

"It was 1 May, Friday morning, and everyone was talking about the riots," said Sergeant Lee. "It was pretty much the only thing on television. Anyway, I was with Third Battalion, First Marines at that time, and we were on what's called air contingency force alert, or ACF.[5] The ACF is poised to respond anywhere Marines might be needed in the world, but we never thought we'd be sent to Los Angeles. Somewhere before noon we got word to load up and move out, *NOW!* I've never seen things move so fast. Our convoy lined up at the Pendleton gate and then off we went up Interstate five.

"On the southbound side of the freeway, traffic was completely stopped. Some people were waving and cheering, while others were staring at us in obvious shock. It was surreal. We were all wearing flak jackets and helmets and carrying M16s. We stopped at the Marine base in Tustin, just outside Los Angeles, and after it got dark we were sent in. Most of the city seemed to be ablaze when we moved into our positions.

"When the city woke up, we were on the streets manning roadblocks and protecting important locations. There was no opportunity for rioters to start looting again, because they were dealing with Marines now. And probably most important, when we did respond to something we responded as one force. Remember, the city was torn apart by racial tension, but here we were, even more diverse than you recruits, working together. We set the example, if you were dealing with a Marine there was no color—we were all green.

"Someone would try to square off against one of us, and we would just come out of the woodwork to back each other up. Just imagine the effect it could have on a community if you twelve were there on the streets, sharing that common bond of being a Marine."

"Were the people hostile toward you, Sergeant?" asked Mascuzzio.

5. ACFs provide air-deployable forces within sixteen hours of notification. They provide a great versatility in that they can fly anywhere in the world to meet maritime pre-positioning ships.

"No, of course not," answered Sergeant Lee. "Some of the punks, yeah, but most of the people in the community were really good. They were so glad to see us that they literally embraced us. They were trapped for all that time by the rioting, so it was almost like we liberated them."

"So no one judged you because of your race?" asked Hill.

"I don't know if I can say that," said Sergeant Lee. "There were some pretty distinct color lines and the racial tension was so thick you could cut it. Much different than what I was used to in the Marines."

The recruits received extensive training on equal opportunity, and would for their entire time in the Corps. The Corps' policy is that all Marines be treated fairly, having equal opportunity regardless of race, ethnicity, age, sex, or religious conviction.

There are several scenarios that drill instructors use to lead guided discussion on fair treatment of all fellow Marines. This educates recruits on how the strength of the Corps is based on mutual concern for each other, and that unfair treatment based on race or ethnicity is un-Marine-like. Simply put, treat everyone with dignity and respect.

13

Night Infiltration Course

The recruits sat in the cold and waited for darkness. This was their first opportunity to take a long break. Removing their boots revealed the source of the pain they felt. Their feet looked like hamburger, with many blisters becoming open wounds. Corpsmen helped to treat the wounds, but, basically, the recruits were expected to take care of themselves.

The temperature dropped low enough for them to feel uncomfortable. As the sun set in the west, it became much cooler than the daytime weather. A breeze from the Pacific Ocean sent shivers through their bodies, leading to their sitting closer together.

Most of the discomfort was because their bodies were drained of energy and were screaming for nutrition. Those who had rationed their food were able to eat something close to a real meal, but most had little food left.

It was 1845 hours. The Crucible would soon be seventeen hours old, leaving another thirty-seven to go. They already had covered more than fifteen miles. For most people this would be the end, with their ability to carry on crushed, but for these soon-to-be-Marines it was just the last portion of their first day.

What awaited the recruits was their first night event—the night infiltration course. It was the same course they'd gone through during the day as part of the endurance course, only now it was pitch black. Again, they crawled under the barbed wire, through the muddy water, and over the walls. Men yelled to each other in the darkness, trying to be heard over the gunfire and explosions. They carried heavy crates of ammunition and supplies with them, suffering as a team during the entire grueling event.

Once completed, the recruits hiked three miles to a bivouac site. With each sloshing step they grew more tired, but the drill instructors would not allow them to forget why they were here. They sang cadence on the return hike, with the drill instructor bellowing a verse that the recruits would repeat:

> Well you can have your Army khakis.
> And you can have your Air Force blues.
> There's a better breed of fighting man.
> I'll introduce to you.
> His uniform is different.
> Than any you've ever seen.
> The Germans call him devil dog.
> His title is Marine.
> He was born at MCRD.
> The land that time forgot.
> The sand was eighteen inches thick.
> The sun was blazing hot . . .

Sergeant Lee sang the cadence with motivation and spirit but he was also feeling tired from the demanding day. Though he had not participated in the obstacles, he still walked everywhere the recruits did and spent even more time on his feet. In addition, the emotional demands of constantly supervising safety procedures and conducting the debriefs of the obstacles contributed to his being exhausted.

The sergeant was able to continue setting the example for several reasons. First, he was an exceptional Marine. Second, he found strength and energy in the recruits' performance and their will to become Marines. Finally, he had been intensely screened and trained to perform the duties of a drill instructor.

From the very beginning, when seasoned privates supervised the training of the new Marines' on-the-job training and rookie squads, enlisted Marines have trained their own. That tradition matured through the decades to create the Marine Corps drill instructor that we see today. When recruit training was formalized in 1911, the training conducted by noncommissioned officers was tough, but not brutal:

> I went through Parris Island when it was supposed to be the old tough Marine Corps [1920]. Nobody ever laid a hand on anybody in my platoon. We didn't have those things happen to us. Most were young men, and were being treated like men. We weren't no-account people who were slapped and kicked."
> —Brig. Gen. Samuel R. Shaw, USMC

Tight budgets of the 1930s led to some privates being assigned as drill instructors. They were not "boots," however. They often had several years of service under their belts. Officers provided little supervision, but the drill instructors did not need to use corporal punishment.

> Drill instructors—they were privates then . . . put my platoon through vigorous training [in 1934] without laying a hand on any of us.[1]
> —Col. M. F. McLane, USMC

The organization and structure of recruit training continued to solidify in the next few decades, along with the training for drill instructors. Drill Instructor School was established in 1942, providing a two-week class on training procedures. The subject matter focused on the information that drill instructors needed to effectively process the huge number of recruits entering the Corps during World War II.

> My drill instructor was a small man. He didn't have a big mouth. He was neither cruel nor sadistic. He was not a bully. But he was a strict disciplinarian, a total realist about our future and an absolute perfectionist dedicated to excellence. To

1. Fleming, Keith, *Corps in Crisis* (South Carolina, South Carolina Press, 1994) 11–13.

him, more than my disciplined home life, a year of college
ROTC, and months of infantry training, I attribute my ability
to have withstood the stress of Peleliu.[2]
—Dr. Eugene Sledge, former Marine Private first class

Until the end of the Korean War, it was not uncommon for new
Marines to be assigned to duty with drill instructors. The best graduates of one platoon would remain on station at the depot to assist
the drill instructors in training the next platoon. This system often
resulted in inappropriate training methods by the young, inexperi-
enced recruit supervisors. No responsible Marine leader condoned
the abuse of Marines, but the system did break down from time to
time.

After the Ribbon Creek tragedy in 1956 came new changes for the
drill instructors and in recruit training. The drill instructor school
became more thorough. There were many other changes: improved
housing, reimbursement for laundry costs, assignment of more commissioned officers, and issuing of the campaign hat.

Originally called the field hat, the campaign cover was first issued
in the 1800s and its official issue was discontinued before World War
II. Marine Corps shooting teams continued to use it for its func-
tionality, making it a trademark for all marksmanship-related activ-
ities. Command Field Sergeant Major at MCRD, Parris Island, MSgt.
W. G. Ferrigno, who was originally issued the cover while undergo-
ing recruit training in 1927, led a campaign to have the field hat
adopted for use by drill instructors. On 21 July 1956, the 21st Commandant, General Pate, directed that it be issued to all drill instructors. The issue was intended to recognize the responsibility entrusted to drill instructors and improve morale within the ranks.

In the mid-1970s, again there was an explosion of public scrutiny
with three separate incidents involving recruits in the space of a few
months. First, a recruit was beaten to death by other recruits during
pugil-stick training in late 1975. Less than two weeks later a recruit

2. Sledge, Eugene, "Peleliu, Neglected Battle," *Marine Corps Gazette,* January 1980. (Quantico, Va., Marine Corps Association.)

died of heat stroke while taking part in a less than one mile march. Finally, in early 1976, a drill instructor shot a recruit in an attempt to frighten him.

The Senate Armed Services Committee conducted an investigation of the Marine Corps' recruiting and recruit-training practices. It found that recruit attrition had risen from 10.5 percent in 1972 to 17.8 percent in 1975 and that recorded incidents of abuse occurred at rates three times higher than other services. Improvements were made in the screening and training of drill instructors, and again additional officers were assigned to the depots.

Today's prospective drill instructor goes through a thorough evaluation process. Headquarters Marine Corps reviews the records of Marines requesting to be drill instructors, and they choose only the best and the brightest to attend Drill Instructor School. They are about twenty-nine years old, in grade of staff sergeant or sergeant, and with about ten years as a Marine. After preliminary headquarters selection the Marine is evaluated by his or her current commanding officer. Those having marital, financial, or other problems are told to apply at a later date. Those who are determined not to be qualified often are told not to reapply. Once applicants have been screened twice, they are sent to San Diego or Parris Island for even more screening to begin.

At Drill Instructor School the prospective drill instructors spend three months learning the skills needed to transform civilians into Marines. Their days are packed with physical training and classes on general military subjects, leadership, the depot's standard operating procedure, and seemingly endless hours on the parade deck practicing close-order drill. Finally, the drill-instructor students complete the Crucible themselves. Some, even those with combat experience, would refer to it as one of the most difficult things they'd ever done.

Their responsibility is to ensure a bright future for the Corps, as was Sergeant Lee's; his creed as a drill instructor demanded this of him:

These recruits are entrusted to my care. I will train them to the best of my ability. I will develop them into smartly disciplined, physically fit, basically trained Marines, thoroughly indoctrinated in love of Corps and Country. I will demand of them, and demonstrate by my own example, the highest standards of personal conduct, morality, and professional skill.

Just words to most, but a commitment for Sergeant Lee and his fellow drill instructors. They do it day in and day out, often fifteen hours a day, for seven days a week. They know that they have the future of the Corps in their hands and a trivial debate over the methods of the past doesn't help the realities of the present.

Incidents of abuse or maltreatment are now isolated incidents that are always handled quickly. A drill-instructor team is supervised by senior staff noncommissioned officers and commissioned officers. The senior Marines are not there to "baby-sit," but to provide guidance in problem areas. It's the same type of chain of command found in all other Marine units.

The key to success of recruit training is the drill instructors. Their commitment has no peacetime equal, and their willingness to drive forward often overwhelms the physical realities of their bodies. As Gen. Robert H. Barrow (commandant 1979 to 1983) said: "My drill instructors lighted a fire in me forty years ago. It's still burning and will until I die."[3]

The recruits finally reached the bivouac site at 2300. Their first taste of sleep was growing closer, but first they would need to clean their weapons, prepare their gear, and tend to their feet in preparation for the next day. If they were lucky, they'd be slumbering by midnight. That is, if they were lucky.

3. Krulak, Victor H., *First to Fight* (Annapolis, Naval Institute Press, 1984) 194.

14

Staff Sergeant Bordelon's Assault

The United States continued to advance across the Pacific during World War II and by 1943 was taking aim at the Japanese home islands. The first step was to take the Gilbert Islands so land-based planes could reach the Marshall Islands chain. The Gilberts consisted of Makin, Tarawa, and Apamama atolls.

Tarawa is a triangular-shaped atoll of islands and reefs, only twelve miles wide and eighteen miles long, about ten feet above sea level at its highest point. The island would have been insignificant if it were not for an A-shaped airfield that occupied the majority of the land. The island was heavily defended, with more than 500 pillboxes, constructed of log, coral, and concrete, designed to impede the Marine attack. The water was also full of obstacles, consisting of mines and barricades that channeled the landing craft into lanes heavily covered by artillery.

On 20 November 1943, Marine amphibious tractors and Higgins boats left their transport ships, headed for the beaches with the 2d Marine Division aboard. They fell short, however, with most caught on the reef surrounding the island. The Marines were forced to wade ashore under brutal fire, with many dying in the water. Some were shot by the enemy, others drowned under their heavy loads. Howitzer crews waded ashore with as much of their heavy equipment as they could carry, covering the 400 meters of watery hell to get to the beach.

Those Marines who made it to the beach found themselves pinned against a log wall by ruthlessly accurate interlocking machine-gun fire. By the end of the first day, 5,000 Marines were ashore holding a small beachhead covering 700 by 300 yards. There were 1,500 casualties. D-day plus one brought more difficulties, as some landing craft spent twenty hours in the water before heading for the beach. On 22 November, Marines supported by tanks swept east and met with savage Japanese counterattacks. The battle raged with grenades, flamethrowers, and bayonets until 23 November. It was the most defiant resistance Marines had encountered on the landing beaches and more than 1,000 men lost their lives.

The Japanese commander of the island stated: "A million Americans could not take Tarawa in a hundred years."[1] The situation for the Marines often seemed hopeless, with units decimated and leaders dead. Only the courage of individual Marines on the beach pushed the battle forward.

"The obstacle that your squad is about to complete is named in honor of William J. Bordelon Jr. He was born on 25 December 1920, in San Antonio, Texas, and enlisted in the Marine Corps on 10 December 1941." Sergeant Lee was tired himself, so he knew the recruits must be about to fall asleep on their feet. The four hours of sleep they had during the night went by too quickly. Before they knew it, they were awake and hiking again. "By 10 July 1942, Bordelon had risen to sergeant and participated in the later stages of Guadalcanal. He landed on Tarawa on D-day and earned the Medal of Honor."

A single telephone pole served as the obstacle for this warrior station. It was about twenty feet high with nothing available to assist one in climbing to the top. It was 0600 on the second day of the Crucible, and although there were only twenty-six hours left, their aches and pains made the end seem like a lifetime away. The recruits were now twenty-eight hours into the Crucible and they had already hiked more than twenty-one miles.

The President of the United States in the name of The Congress takes pleasure in presenting the Medal of Honor posthumously to Staff Sergeant William J. Bordelon, United States Marine Corps, for service set forth in the following citation:

1. Alexander, Joseph H., *A Fellowship of Valor: The Battle History of the United States Marines* (New York, HarperCollins, 1997) 41.

For valorous and gallant conduct above and beyond the call of duty as a member of an assault engineer platoon of the 1st Battalion, 18th Marines, tactically attached to the 2d Marine Division, in action against the Japanese-held atoll of Tarawa in the Gilbert Islands on 20 November 1943. Landing in the assault waves under withering enemy fire which killed all but four of the men in his tractor, Staff Sergeant Bordelon hurriedly made demolition charges and personally put two pillboxes out of action. Hit by enemy machine-gun fire just as a charge exploded in his hand while assaulting a third position, he courageously remained in action and, although out of demolitions, provided himself with a rifle and furnished fire coverage for a group of men scaling the seawall. Disregarding his own serious condition, he unhesitatingly went to the aid of one of his demolition men, wounded and calling for help in the water, rescuing this man and another who had been hit by enemy fire while attempting to make the rescue. Still refusing first aid for himself, he again made up demolition charges and singlehanded assaulted a fourth Japanese machine-gun position but was instantly killed when caught in a final burst of fire from the enemy. Staff Sergeant Bordelon's great personal valor during a critical phase of securing the limited beachhead was a contributing factor in the ultimate occupation of the island and his heroic determination throughout three days of violent battle reflects the highest credit upon the United States Naval Service. He gallantly gave his life for his country. Signed, Franklin D. Roosevelt[2]

Stomachs rumbled painfully for food. So far the recruits had missed four full meals, so many drank as much water as they could to reduce the effects of the hunger. Little by little the contents of their two-and-a-half meals had disappeared, with many realizing that

2. Medal of Honor citation from *The Congressional Medal of Honor, The Names, The Deeds* (Chico, Calif., Sharp and Dunnigan, 1988) 268.

they would soon be completely out of food. To get some calories for energy they were eating the sugar packages that came with the MREs.

"Staff Sergeant Bordelon was twenty-two years old and was wounded multiple times before he was killed. He was originally buried on Tarawa, but on the fifty-second anniversary of the Tarawa battle, the citizens of San Antonio brought him back home. For two days and nights his casket lay in state in the Alamo, surrounded by a Marine honor guard."

"Can I be the leader for this one, Sergeant?" asked Evans.

"Why?" said Sergeant Lee, smiling.

"Because he's from Texas, Sergeant," answered Evans. Evans was a decent recruit, but Sergeant Lee could already see that he had a difficult life ahead of him. There was a girl back home pregnant by him. She was only nineteen, barely out of high school. Evans decided that military service was the only way he could get the medical benefits needed for a family. The future wouldn't be as bright as he thought, however. With a child and wife, at least until he became a corporal, he would probably live below the poverty line. There were no easy answers, because it was a complicated life that faced them. Marriage, youth, and the Marine Corps did not make an easy mix.

"Very well, you're the leader," said Sergeant Lee. "I think Staff Sergeant Bordelon would have wanted a fellow Texan to take charge during his obstacle."

"Aye, aye, Sergeant," said Evans.

"Here's your situation. Your company is pinned down by fire from an enemy bunker. Your squad has maneuvered to a ventilation shaft leading into the bunker and you have one demolition charge. Your mission is to destroy the bunker by lowering the demolition charge into the ventilation shaft. You will have a truck tire to represent the charge."

Sergeant Lee pointed to an old tire on the ground. The recruits had to find a way to get to the top of the pole and get the tire around it. To do this they built another human pyramid and handed the tire up to the man on top. Then, they lowered the tire down the "shaft" to the base of the pole, setting it on the ground.

"We're all done, Sergeant," said Evans.

"Are you? While you were lowering the demolition charge into the bunker, other men from your company entered and secured it. So now you have to retrieve the demolition charge from the ventilation shaft." *Easy enough*, thought the recruits. They just put it on the pole with little trouble. "But, you can't be in the same position as you were before. If you were on top, you now have to be on the bottom."

When the recruits originally put the tire over the pole the largest recruits naturally were on the bottom of the pyramid. Now the smaller recruits would need to get on the bottom, and the larger ones would stand on them. Throwing another challenge at the recruits was necessary to remind them that the unexpected was often the most difficult type of adversity to deal with.

The second human pyramid was a miserable sight. The small recruits had a difficult time holding the weight of the larger ones, who were now stacked two high on their shoulders. Griping and complaints began, but this time several men put an end to it themselves. There was no yelling, just a reminder that they needed to stay motivated and work together.

Time ran out before they could get the tire off the pole. Sergeant Lee told them to use the original pyramid to remove it so the next group would be able to start the obstacle. They had failed, a not unexpected situation, as several times recruits were put into "no-win" situations. The recruits had demonstrated that they learned several important lessons from their mistakes earlier in the Crucible. Although they were tired and this was the most likely time for arguments to begin, they stayed focused on the task at hand and did the best they could. All too often, battles were won by the men in the unit who remained faithful to one another.

"What happened, why couldn't you get the tire back off?"

"Those of us little guys on the bottom couldn't hold Hill and Simms and the others," said Nushi.

"I think we would have got it with just a little bit more time," said Evans.

"I think you're probably right, but how did you work as a team?"

"We did a lot better than we have on some of the other stations," said Smith.

"I think you're right. I was impressed with the way you stayed motivated and tried to work together when it was so easy to complain instead."

"It's getting easier to suck it up and drive on," said Simms. "Especially when you think about what Staff Sergeant Bordelon did."

"Marines like him are the whole reason we were successful in the Pacific during World War II. The Japanese commander of the island said that it couldn't be taken in a hundred years, but we did it in three days. It wasn't cheap, however, as a thousand Marines died there. Many of them had to wade ashore when their landing craft got caught on the coral reef. That's one of the reasons why we took you to the pool in first phase to teach you how to swim."

Recruit swim training took place during the fifth week of training. It was intended to give the recruit the basic skills needed to survive in the water. At the very least, each man jumped from a ten-foot tower while in camouflage uniform, swam fifty meters, treaded water for two minutes, demonstrated a survival float for one minute, and remove their trousers to inflate and use as a flotation device.

"In November of 1995, a Marine lance corporal fell off an aircraft carrier into the Arabian Sea. No one saw him fall, and because an aircraft carrier holds more than 5,000 men and women, it took time before he was reported missing. Searchers were unable to locate him, so he had to save himself. He stayed afloat for more than thirty-six hours by using the training he'd received. He inflated his trousers to use them for flotation and refused to quit. A Pakistani fishing boat found him floating unconscious in the water and rescued him. When they made land, the Marine located the only telephone in the village, and called his parents who were worried because they were informed that he was missing at sea. The parents then called the Marine Corps to tell them that he was safe."

Sergeant Lee finished the debrief by reviewing the definition of commitment, with special emphasis on unselfishness. He related Staff Sergeant Bordelon's actions to how good Marines take care of fellow Marines and their families before themselves.

15

Corporal Laville's Duty

The first female to call herself "Marine" was Lucy Brewer. In the War of 1812, she served on the USS *Constitution* under the name George Baker. Women first served, officially, as United States Marines during World War I, when 305 "Reservists (Female)" became clerks in uniform to "Free a Marine to fight." Opha Mae Johnson became the first woman to enlist in the Marine Corps on 13 August 1918. It was a remarkable opportunity for women, especially considering that it wasn't until 26 August 1920 that the Nineteenth Amendment granted American women the right to vote. Immediately following the war, however, the commandant ordered all women out of the reserves, and the Corps became an all-male institution again.

During World War II, the Marine Corps Women's Reserve (MCWR) was established again and more than 18,000 women joined. Women officers were appointed, with Maj. Ruth Cheney Streeter (retired as a colonel in 1945) becoming the director of the MCWR. Women served in more than two hundred different jobs during the war: pilot, airplane mechanic, parachute rigger, photographer, cryptographer, gunnery instructor, air-traffic controller, and naval air navigator. By war's end, 85 percent of the enlisted Marines assigned to Headquarters Marine Corps were women. Eighteen members of the MCWR died of various causes during the war.

Their service continued after the war, but most were limited to duty as reservists. A small number remained on active duty to serve as a nucleus during mobilization. In 1948, President Truman signed the Women's Armed Services Integration Act, which allowed women to serve in the regular forces. Recruit training for females began in

1949 at Parris Island, and Capt. Margaret M. Henderson became the first commanding officer of the new female recruit-training battalion. The first platoon was formed on 2 March 1949,[1] and SSgts. Dorothy Sullivan and Betty Schultz became the first female drill instructors. The Women's Officer Training Class was established in Quantico in June of that same year, and Capt. Elise Hill was named as its commander.

During the Korean War, as with other wars, women were not drafted into the military, although there was a proposal to do so. The need for men to fight overseas led to the number of women in the Corps rising to about 6,500. In 1953, SSgt. Barbara Barnwell was the first woman to receive the Navy and Marine Corps Medal (highest award for heroism awarded to a Marine or sailor for noncombat action) when she saved the life of a drowning Marine in the Atlantic.

Geraldine Moran became the first female sergeant major in 1960. In 1965, SSgt. Josephine Gebers was the first to serve under fire in the Dominican Republic. The Vietnam War also led to more occupational specialties being opened to women. Master Sergeant Barbara Dulinsky was the first female Marine to report for duty in Vietnam in 1967. A total of twenty-eight enlisted women and eight women officers served in Vietnam; three were awarded the Bronze Star.

In 1975, women were authorized to serve in all occupational fields except ground combat, pilot, and air crew. On 11 May 1978, Margaret Brewer became the first female general officer in the Corps' history.

In the mid-1980s women began to serve in the Marine Corps Security Battalion assigned to duty at American embassies and consulates around the world. Two were on duty, dressed in helmets and flak jackets and armed with shotguns and pistols, when the American consulate in Karachi, Pakistan, was rushed by thousands of Pakistani demonstrators during November 1979.

In the Gulf War, approximately 1,000 women served in a variety of combat support billets, and four women communicators passed

---

1. Women received entry-level training before this date, but it was not officially considered "recruit training."

through the breach of Iraqi defenses on G-day of Desert Storm to earn the Combat Action Ribbon. The first Marine from 2d Force Service Support Group to be recommended for a Bronze Star in the Gulf War was a woman.

In June 1992, Brig. Gen. Carol Mutter[2] became the first woman to command a Fleet Marine Force unit at the flag-rank level. The following year, in July 1993, 2d Lt. Sarah Deal became the first woman Marine selected for flight school. She earned her wings on 21 April 1995 and later served as a CH-53E helicopter pilot. The Marines got their first female fighter pilot in October 1997, when 1st Lt. Karen Tribbett received her flight wings as an F-18 pilot.

Today, enlisted women undergo segregated recruit training at Parris Island in the 4th Recruit Training Battalion. They are trained by female drill instructors, who also wear the campaign cover, and are supervised by female officers. The training of men and women is segregated to provide an opportunity for socialization within the Corps before integration between the sexes. Marine Corps Recruit Training is a dramatic shock to any young American, regardless of gender. Segregation removes the distracting sexual undercurrent often present in a coeducational setting. The training for the women is similar to that of the males, with females also participating in the Crucible as well.

Women Marines now receive combat training and graduate from many formerly male-only schools. They are also found in a growing number of military occupational specialties and participating in shipboard deployments.

"This obstacle is named in honor of Germaine Catherine Laville, born on 16 May 1922, in Plaquemine, Louisiana. She graduated from Louisiana State University and was working as a teacher in her

2. General Mutter was later promoted to the rank of lieutenant general, becoming the first female three-star general in the Corps and the second ever in the United States military, quite an accomplishment considering that women make up only 5 percent of the Corps, and the Corps is the smallest of the services.

hometown during World War II. There were no men of draft age in her family, so she decided to become part of the war effort by enlisting in July of 1943. She chose the Marine Corps because of its reputation as an elite fighting force and was assigned as an instructor because of her experience and education as a teacher."

0635 and nearing hour number twenty-nine. The obstacle was one of the more complex designs, with six tires suspended by cables, positioned seven feet apart.

Citation: Laville's primary duty was as an aerial gunnery instructor in a large two-story structure called the Synthetic Training Building (STB). On Saturday, 3 June 1944, more than fifty Marines were preparing to change duty shifts in the STB. Nine civilian cleaning men were also at work waxing the floors. At 2:51 P.M., the highly volatile liquid floor wax thrown by a buffing machine hit the worn wires of a flight simulation machine, in effect setting the entire first floor corridor and lobby ablaze. The devastating fire consumed the wooden building within minutes. Five Marines died and thirty-seven were injured. Corporal Laville was last seen inside the burning building and gave her life trying to help others escape. Corporal Laville's life of twenty-two years was exemplified by altruistic behavior and devotion to others. Her military service and ultimate sacrifice have become legend in her hometown of Iberville Parish, Louisiana, and at Louisiana State University. Although Corporal Laville did not receive a Medal of Honor, she is commemorated for her unselfish patriotic service to her country, and her fellow Marines.

Sergeant Lee assigned a recruit named Puckett as the leader for this obstacle. At nineteen Puckett joined to follow the footsteps of his father who died during a training exercise when he was young.

"Your squad has secured the top floor of a building. The building has caught fire and the only way out is to cross to a neighboring building. There are cables suspended between the two buildings. You estimate that the fire will reach you in twenty-five minutes. Your mission is to move your squad and your equipment from the burning building to the safety of the adjacent building.

"Coordinating instructions: One, if a team member or piece of gear touches the ground it is eliminated from the problem. Two, only one team member on a tire at a time. Are there any questions?"

Puckett was not a forceful leader, so other recruits developed the plan they used to overcome the obstacle. They needed to swing from tire to tire, timing their movements so the others would be able to catch the tire on its backward swing. This obstacle looked fun and was at first, but about halfway through, their forearms and biceps began to burn from fatigue. Many needed to rest, hanging onto the tire while the others behind them suffered. Several recruits lost their grips and fell to the ground.

Those having problems received words of encouragement, but none of the recruits who had completed the tiring crossing went back to help them. Sergeant Lee wrote a note to remember to discuss it during the debrief. He was tired, so his notes ensured that he didn't forget to cover important points of the recruits' performance.

Time ran out and several recruits "died." Three had fallen to the ground, with two stranded on the "burning" side of the obstacle because those in front had taken too long in crossing. For the debrief Lee split them into three groups: those who made the crossing, those who fell, and those who didn't finish.

"How did we do as a team, Puckett?" asked Sergeant Lee.

"We did a good job of passing the tires back and forth, and not complaining, but we still didn't do it."

"There wasn't enough time," said Simms.

"So there isn't anything that might have been better in your teamwork?"

The recruits didn't answer, but their body language expressed the belief that they had done everything they could.

"Why didn't you go back for the other recruits when they were having problems?" Sergeant Lee asked of the recruits who'd completed the crossing to safety. "They were out there trying to swing to get momentum to grab the next tire and all of you could have helped."

"I didn't know that we could, Sergeant," said Puckett.

"The rules didn't say that we could do that," said Simms.

"Did it say that you couldn't?" The recruits looked at each other, but didn't answer. "Did anyone tell Corporal Laville that she could go back in the fire and save others?"

"No, Sergeant," said Nushi. "She used her initiative and did it on her own."

"More people might have died if she had waited," said Waters.

"So she was committed, wasn't she?"

"Yes, Sergeant," answered the squad.

"Her commitment to her country led to joining the Marine Corps, and the courage that she showed during the fire likely saved lives. She joined for the same reasons most of us did, because the Marine Corps is an elite fighting force. Her example should have led you to go back after your buddies."

Women are an integral part of the Marine Corps, meaning these men would serve with them wherever they are stationed. They came from all walks of life, making it necessary for the Marine Corps to ensure each was thoroughly educated on proper behavior. Recruits receive extensive training on sexual harassment. They are taught that sexual harassment included influencing, offering to influence, or threatening the career, pay, or job of another person in exchange for sexual favors. Also banned are the deliberate or repeated offensive comments or jokes, gestures, or physical conduct of a sexual nature.

The policy is clear: Sexual harassment is unacceptable and unprofessional behavior for military or civilian personnel and is dealt with through leadership and the chain of command. Leaders and supervisors have a dual responsibility to create and to maintain an environment of mutual respect in which men and women can function effectively.

As with the racism-guided discussions, there are several scenarios used by drill instructors to lead guided discussions on proper treatment of fellow Marines regardless of sex. The message was clear: Treat all with dignity and respect.

16

Combat Course

The next few obstacles combined to represent a combatlike scenario. First, the recruits ran through a standard Marine Corps obstacle course, with all of their gear, while carrying a stretcher with a heavy dummy (90 pounds) representing a "wounded" Marine in need of help. The obstacle course required them to crawl over a series of logs and poles to a twenty-foot rope, which was to be climbed at the end.

They were next told that the rest of their platoon needed help in defending against an enemy attack some three miles away. They had to don the packs, tighten their boots, and step off on a forced march to reinforce the other men. Normally, the three miles would pose a minuscule challenge, but it became difficult after twenty-nine hours of almost continuous operations with little food and sleep. The squad barely completed it within the time limit. They now had hiked twenty-four miles and missed four meals, but they were more than half complete with the Crucible.

As soon as the recruits arrived at their destination, they were given live ammunition for their M16A2 service rifles and ordered to move forward to hasty positions where they could engage the enemy. They deployed and began to fire at the targets in front of them in the range's impact area. The targets fell when hit, so they knocked them all down using marksmanship and clean weapons. Otherwise, they would have failed in their mission by not placing well-aimed shots, or maintaining their weapons properly, because the enemy would have remained standing.

When the recruits had fired all of their ammunition, the drill instructors designated several "casualties" for them to evacuate. The casualties were told to scream as if they were in pain and the drill instructors started interjecting stress into the situation by yelling at the recruits. The pressure they experienced would not be the same as if a buddy's life were threatened, but it did add more stress to the training event. The squad carried the "wounded" recruits about a mile to a medical evacuation site.

The squad had gone through a forced march to reinforce their platoon, engaged the enemy with live ammunition, and evacuated several wounded men. Now they were to experience close combat. The men donned football helmets and other protective clothing to fight each other with pugil sticks, padded to look like a big Q-tip and simulate a rifle. The men used them to fight mock bayonet battles.

Another squad was waiting to fight them, in bouts of two men on two. When one was "killed" with a blow to the head, the survivor fought outnumbered two to one. The recruits fought three separate bouts, one after another with no breaks. Each lasted several minutes, completely exhausting the recruits by the time they were over. The rotation of fights was arranged so that the first fight was against two recruits on their third fight. Fight number two was an even match, with each group on their second fight. The final fight was against a fresh team. This led to the recruits having to fight two less exhausted men when they were the most tired. The fights only became harder as the recruits became weaker.

This training needs to be tough to prepare recruits for the future. Marines are expected to be most ready when the nation is least ready, performing duties the president directs. Recruits who graduated in the decade prior found themselves in harm's way shortly after claiming the title Marine. They served all over the world: Liberia, Kuwait, Iraq, the Philippines, Bangladesh, Somalia, Haiti, Cuba, Bosnia, Rwanda, the Persian Gulf, Adriatic Sea, Central African Republic, and Albania. They also served humanitarian operations in the United States during riots, fires, earthquakes, floods, and hurricanes.

The missions of the future will demand new skills of Marines. The Crucible Event is a response to uncertainty, because Marines need to be trained to handle any situation with which they are faced. They may have to evacuate civilians or kill a deadly enemy. For these and other situations they need to be smart, disciplined, and tough. This is nothing new for Marines; the Crucible is simply a new way of achieving it.

Immediately following the pugil-stick bouts, the recruits hiked to another reaction course. Now that they were extremely tired, they had to be put in a situation that required them to think. This highlighted the impact of fatigue on decision making.

At the first station the squad was advancing to a hill where they could observe the enemy and call in artillery fire to support an infantry attack. They encountered a minefield and an obstacle designed to stop a tank. The limits of the enemy barricade was unknown and there was no time to breach it. The laser range-finder equipment they had, represented by a fifty-five-gallon drum, needed to be put into position quickly.

The squad immediately broke into three different teams, with one providing security, another beginning to scout a route through the barrier, and the last preparing the barrel for movement. A human chain was set up in places with no mines, so the barrel could be passed through the minefield and over the obstacle. The squad members followed when the barrel was on the other side, successfully accomplishing their mission.

Next, the squad was carrying vital medical supplies to a badly mauled unit. A small bridge over a dangerously swift river was blown up by the enemy earlier in the day, but some of the bridge supports remained. Not all the charges detonated, leaving some portions of the bridge vulnerable to further explosions. The medical supplies were needed across the river for the other unit immediately.

Careful to avoid the unexploded charges, the men laid across the remaining supports and formed a human bridge. The medical supplies were carried by the lighter members of the squad, and they worked their way across without losing any men.

The squad's next mission was setting explosives in an enemy communication facility. Their progress was impeded by a double fence, with the one nearest them booby trapped and the area between the two fences mined. If they touched the near fence or the ground behind it they would be killed. Enemy patrols were in the area and would probably pass in about twenty minutes. The recruits needed to get into the compound to set the demolitions, so their company could use the surprise to launch an attack. They found a pile of junk (pipes, ropes, and boxes) that they could use.

The recruits were completely stumped by the difficult problem. They had no idea where to begin, until Smith suggested building an A-frame from the pipes. The A-frame was slightly higher than the first fence, allowing them to place a pole on it. The pole was then placed on the top of the second fence, creating an awkward and unstable crossing. The majority of the squad stabilized the A-frame so Nushi and Northwood could climb over the first fence and minefield without touching them. Unfortunately, they ran out of time and failed before they could accomplish the mission.

At the last station, the squad was en route to resupply their platoon with radio batteries. A bridge crossing a river was destroyed by artillery, but some rubble still remained. The squad had twenty minutes to get itself and the batteries across. They had three planks they could use.

From the beginning it was obvious that none of the planks were long enough to make it between the gaps in the rubble. To get across, the recruits used a counterbalance, placing several heavy recruits at one end of a plank so another could walk out on the unsupported end. Every action was carefully thought out and discussed, and consequences were reviewed thoroughly. Meticulously the recruits crossed the gaps, barely making it across within the time limit.

Sergeant Lee used lessons from the combat course and various Medal of Honor citations during the debriefs, combining decision making and combat as best he could. For example, he related the pugil sticks to Sergeant Cukela's actions and his decision to use captured grenades to destroy other German machine-gun positions. He also discussed Staff Sergeant Howard's decision to distribute his ammunition and drag a radio around the perimeter calling in fire missions when he was unable to walk.

The recruits were almost completely drained of energy and such stories provided both inspiration and a reminder of how small their challenges were. They were hurting, but would succeed by relying on each other. It was a little past 1300 when they started their next hike and twenty-fifth mile. The sun was high, with the heat virtually unendurable to the drained men. But still, they continued to move further in the Crucible.

17

Lance Corporal Noonan's Casualty Evacuation

Richard Nixon entered the White House in 1969 during the Vietnam War and soon decided on the "Vietnamization" of the war. He planned to gradually remove American forces from that conflict. The Corps then numbered 314,000 throughout the world and battles still continued to rage in Vietnam.

Operation Dewey Canyon (22 January to 19 March) had the 9th Marine Regiment spending almost a full two months in the field attacking communist camps near the Laotian border. It was a completely helicopter-supported operation, with the helos even transporting artillery pieces to support the infantry. Monsoons complicated the already difficult logistical challenges of the operation, and so would enemy 122mm mortars and antiaircraft weapons. Leapfrogging from mountaintop to mountaintop, the shifting artillery fire-support bases proved essential to the success of the infantrymen on the ground. For example, a single rifle company was able to ambush a larger enemy force on the Ho Chi Minh trail. Overall, Dewey Canyon was one of the best Marine operations of the war.

The Tet holiday came and went with only a fraction of the violence experienced a year prior. The enemy infiltrated into Da Nang and the surrounding countryside, however, and stepped up other operations along the border. Again, Marines fought with distinction and the enemy was quickly routed. A total of 25,000 Americans left Vietnam in August, but 1,051 Marines were killed and 9,286 were wounded during 1969.

Things would slow down for the Corps in 1970. 12,900 Marines left Vietnam by April, leaving approximately 21,000 in-country.

Their primary duty was to protect Da Nang. The Corps suffered 403 killed and 3,625 wounded during the year.

More would leave Vietnam in 1971 until there were only 13,600 formed into a single brigade. The combined action platoons were disbanded and the control of many areas completely slipped to the communists. Marines continued the work started by Lieutenant Colonel Croizat in 1954, serving as advisors to Vietnamese units.

In late March 1972, the 500 Marines left in-country were instrumental in defeating a major North Vietnamese assault. Very brave Marine advisors, or "Covans," never left the side of their Vietnamese counterparts. They used massive amounts of American air and naval gunfire support to stop the offensive north of Hue.

By early 1973, all troops were gone from Vietnam and America's longest war was over. Though billions in military equipment was left for the South Vietnamese Army, it wasn't enough. In March 1975, the North Vietnamese Army, well trained and armed with Soviet weapons, pushed all the way to the outskirts of Saigon. About the same time, neighboring Cambodia fell to the communist-led Khmer Rouge. Marines helped in evacuation of both embassies, pulling more than 7,000 people from the two countries during the month of April. In May, as an ugly ending to their Southeast Asia experience, Marines were involved in an ill-fated mission to rescue the crew of the unarmed American container ship *Mayaguez*. The Marines landed by helicopter on the Cambodian island of Koh Tang, only to find a determined enemy and no hostages. Only through the valiant efforts of brave Air Force helicopter pilots, the Marines were extracted from the island under withering enemy fire.

Vietnam was the Marine Corps' costliest war. A total of 13,067 Marines died and 88,633 were wounded in action. Although Marines were only one-tenth of all American forces that served in Vietnam, one of every four names on the Vietnam Memorial is a Marine. Fifty-seven were awarded the Medal of Honor, each a story of personal sacrifice and dedication to fellow Marines.

"This obstacle is named in honor of Thomas F. Noonan," said Sergeant Lee. "He was born on 18 November 1943, in Brooklyn, New York, graduated with a bachelor's degree in June of 1966 from Hunter College. He could have received a commission in any of the services, but he decided to enlist in the Marine Corps as an infantryman in December 1967. He reported to Vietnam in July 1968 for service with the 9th Marines. Noonan earned the Medal of Honor during Operation Dewey Canyon in 1969."

It was now 1340 and the recruits were about to enter their thirty-sixth hour of operations. With five full meals missed and twenty-six miles walked, they could feel that the end was near. There were only eighteen hours to go; their desire to be Marines moved them forward.

The President of the United States in the name of The Congress takes pleasure in presenting the Medal of Honor posthumously to Lance Corporal Thomas P. Noonan Jr., United States Marine Corps, for service set forth in the following citation:

> For conspicuous gallantry and intrepidity at the risk of his life above and beyond the call of duty while serving as a Fire Team Leader with Company G, 2d Battalion, 9th Marines, 3d Marine Division, in operations against the enemy in Quang Tri Province in the Republic of Vietnam. On 5 February 1969, Company G was directed to move from a position which they had been holding southeast of the Vandergrift Combat Base in the A Shau Valley to an alternate location. As the Marines commenced a slow and difficult descent down the side of the hill, made extremely slippery by the heavy rains, the leading element came under a heavy fire from a North Vietnamese army unit occupying well-concealed positions in the rocky terrain. Four men were wounded, and repeated attempts to recover them failed because of the intense hostile fire. Lance Corporal Noonan moved from his position of relative security and, maneuvering down the treacherous slope to a location near the injured men, took cover behind some rocks. Shouting words of encouragement to the wounded men to restore their confidence, he dashed across the hazardous terrain and commenced dragging the most seriously wounded man away from the fire-swept area. Although wounded and knocked to the ground by an enemy round, Lance Corporal Noonan recovered rapidly and resumed dragging the man toward the marginal security

of a rock. He was, however, mortally wounded before he could reach his destination. His heroic actions inspired his fellow Marines to such aggressiveness that they initiated a spirited assault which forced the enemy soldiers to withdraw. Lance Corporal Noonan's indomitable courage, inspiring initiative, and selfless devotion to duty upheld the highest traditions of the Marine Corps and the United States Naval Service. He gallantly gave his life for his country. Signed, Richard M. Nixon[1]

By default, Martinez became the leader of the recruit squad. He was the last of the twelve recruits who had not served as a squad leader on a warrior station. In his earlier life, he tried hard to be a tough guy, and might have been, but here he was just another recruit. He had what Sergeant Lee thought was the worst homemade tattoo ever seen on Marine Corps Recruit Depot, San Diego across his stomach: big crooked letters that spelled out MARTINEZ. He enlisted from the Chicago area in an attempt to get away from the streets, proving that he was smart. He realized that he wasn't going anywhere in life unless he made something happen.

There was no physical obstacle constructed for this warrior station. Several stretchers lay before the squad and it was obvious that they would be carrying someone in them. They could barely carry themselves forward, and the thought of carrying another "wounded" buddy posed a huge obstacle.

"Your unit has been ambushed by an enemy force. You need to move the casualties to the landing point for a medical evacuation by helicopter. It will be at the landing zone in thirty minutes." Sergeant Lee appointed Simms and Hill to be the "wounded" men. They were the heaviest in the squad, making things that much harder for the other recruits. "Your mission is to evacuate the injured team members and ensure that they reach safety."

Martinez organized the ten remaining recruits into two teams to start out on the course. Four were on each stretcher, leaving two men

1. Medal of Honor citation from *The Congressional Medal of Honor, The Names, The Deeds* (Chico, Calif., Sharp and Dunnigan, 1988) 120.

who walked along with the others to "rest." The amount of rest was relative, however, because each carried one of the two heavy ammunition cans Sergeant Lee gave to the squad. There would be no escape from the pain of a heavy load.

The recruits worked exceptionally well together, everyone rotating between the ammunition cans and the stretchers with absolutely no complaining. They found strength from each others' will to participate and help the teams move their wounded comrades. They walked several hundred meters, stopped, switched sides to use a different arm, and moved forward for another several hundred meters. The progress was fast, and the recruits finished the obstacle in just over twenty minutes.

"That was darn good," said Sergeant Lee. He was surprised, but really shouldn't have been. He'd trained them himself and they'd become a direct reflection of his example. "How did the load feel?"

"Heavy, Sergeant," laughed Waters.

"There was no getting away from it," said Martinez. "Either it was the stretcher or the ammunition cans, so the only thing to do was drive forward and get it over with."

"Do you think that's what motivated Lance Corporal Noonan?" asked Sergeant Lee.

"Probably not, Sergeant," said Smith. "Whereas he went from a safe position to a painful and dangerous one, we did the opposite."

"It was in our best interest to get to the end," said Simms. "We were doing what was best for us. Lance Corporal Noonan was thinking of everyone but himself."

"So we do notice the difference. On the surface it might seem that we've done something great by getting through this quickly. Don't get me wrong, you did well, but it can't compare to what Lance Corporal Noonan did. He acted as Marines have for decades, always willing to risk everything to take care of another Devil Dog. But, tell me, would we have worked as hard if the person on the stretcher were dead?"

On the morning of 19 April 1995, the Murrah Federal Building in Oklahoma City was blown up by a bomb. The blast nearly collapsed the entire building, and the downtown area of the city was thrust into a hellish day of death and suffering.

Several Marines would be recognized as heroes for their performance after the bombing. Captain Matthew Cooper and Sgt. Tad Snidecor of Recruiting Station, Oklahoma City, received the Navy and Marine Corps Medal for heroism. Both were on the sixth floor of the building when the bomb exploded. They were injured, but were still able to help other survivors out of the building. Once outside, they dug with their hands to pull survivors from the blast. Two of the 167 dead were fellow Marines: Capt. Randolph Guzman and Sgt. Benjamin Davis. Cooper and Snidecor could not find them, but one of their bodies would be removed by brother Marines days later.

Hundreds of police officers and firefighters from across the country were activated under the Federal Emergency Management Agency (FEMA) and sent to Oklahoma City. For the first forty hours none rested, pushing aside the psychological trauma caused by the explosion.

Michael Curtain, New York City police officer, was part of the rescue operation. Spent of energy and moving forward only on the hope that there still might be people alive in the rubble, he came across a body wearing deep blue trousers with a broad red stripe—*Blood Stripe!*[2] Being a Marine Reserve first sergeant with fourteen years of active duty experience, he immediately knew he had just found one of the two missing Marines. Curtain correctly identified the victim as Captain Guzman, the executive officer of the recruiting station.

As word that a Marine had been found circulated through the rescue teams, others who had once worn the Marine uniform came to assist Curtain in his efforts. When concern about the unstable structure threatened to halt the recovery of Captain Guzman's body, these prior service Marines requested to continue their unique mission despite the danger. After nearly five hours of difficult and risky work they removed the captain's body from the rubble, insisting that it be done with due honor and respect.

2. Worn on the blue dress uniform of officers and noncommissioned officers to commemorate the Marine blood shed at Chapultepec and the Halls of Montezuma, 1847.

An Air Force officer provided an American flag that they draped over Guzman's body and word spread throughout the downtown area that Marines were bringing out one of their own. Cranes stopped, quiet fell on the area, people removed their hats and bowed their heads as the workers formed a corridor for the dead Marine. "When we came out with the flag-draped captain, I saw why I was a Marine," said Vietnam veteran and former corporal Manny Hernandez. "It is because I wouldn't expect anything else from any other Marine if it were me in that body bag. It was overwhelming. We are a band of brothers. Once we saw that blood stripe, we knew it was a Marine—we had no choice. It was simply *Semper Fidelis!*"[3]

Sergeant Lee told the story to the recruits, but he needed to pause halfway through. There were no tears, no quivering lip, only a long, poignant silence. Each time he told this story it affected him as it struck an emotional chord. Although some might think it was a sign of weakness, he was not ashamed that the recruits saw his emotion. By this time, they understood.

"For three months I've been trying to teach you how to be Marines. I cannot teach you what it *feels* like to be a Marine, but I think you just saw it. In any other group I would probably be embarrassed, because most people wouldn't understand how I could find something special in a story about a bunch of middle-aged men trying to remove a body.

"I don't know any of the Marines in that story, but I know what motivated their actions. When you find yourself in harm's way, patriotism and political rhetoric mean little. As in the case of Lance Corporal Noonan, in the end, it will always be for each other.

"We don't have the Crucible to make you better than the Marines who have built our Corps' legend. That's impossible. What we want to do is ensure that you are as much like them as possible, willing to carry the battle forward in the face of extreme adversity. We want you to fight as they did so that our country's future shines as brightly as our past."

3. Jenks, Robert, "Two Marines Die in Oklahoma Blast," *Leatherneck* (Quantico, Va., Marine Corps Association, June 1995.)

18

Confidence Course

The confidence course provided the recruits with yet another daunting challenge. It was designed to put the men in situations that force them to face fear. The obstacles required high climbs, and even those with no apprehension about heights might have naturally experienced fright. Most obstacles were nothing new, as the recruits had trained on them in earlier training phases. But now there were additional requirements and limitations, creating a challenge that could only be accomplished by a group working together.

It was 1430 and the recruits now could claim more than twenty-six marching miles. The past thirty-seven hours were, of course, a complete blur. There had been so many obstacles, so many challenges, so many times that they thought they couldn't continue on. Time no longer existed for them as they moved forward instinctively, as was instilled in them by the drill instructors. There was no food left and the lack of sleep had reduced their ability to think and make quick and accurate decisions. Although each was past the point where he thought he could continue, nobody quit.

Now that they were tired and overstressed both emotionally and physically, the chance of fear dominating the individual or the group increased, as in combat. Skills to help overcome fear do not come naturally, but are the result of intensive training. The effects on fear of sleep deprivation, poor diet, and poor hygiene need to be understood through experience for Marines to be ready for battle. Tough training like the Crucible produced more effective combat units and fewer casualties on the battlefield caused by panic or mistakes.

The first obstacle was the stairway to heaven, an oversized ladder with twelve rungs spaced three to four feet apart. Several portions of the rungs are painted red, which means they cannot be touched by the recruits. Smith climbed to the top of the ladder and hooked a rope to a D ring so that heavy radio batteries could be pulled up and over the top. The recruits on the ground formed a mule team and pulled the weight of the load to the top of the ladder. Smith struggled to lift the weight over the last rung, and Simms had to climb to the top to help him. The two were finally able to manipulate it over the top and lower it to the other side of the obstacle. Overall, it was easy compared to the other Crucible challenges, but it was just the beginning of the confidence course.

The skyscraper was a three-story building with no walls. The vertical support beams were slightly slanted in an outward direction, making it nearly impossible for one person to climb to the next level without assistance. Every recruit climbed to the top with all of his gear and rifle where there was a heavy mannequin simulating a Marine who'd been shot by a sniper. Nushi was having a lot of difficulty due to a slight fear of heights. The example and encouragement of the others made stopping impossible, and Waters took special interest in seeing that Nushi always had a solid hand to pull him to the next level of the skyscraper. Waters knew what it was like to need encouragement, so he was more than willing to offer it. The recruits administered first aid and then lowered their "wounded" comrade to the ground. To do this they created a human chain on a cargo net running along the back side of the obstacle, handing the mannequin down one man to the next. Each then climbed down the awkward net to the ground.

On the "monkey" bridge the squad was tasked with carrying valuable medical supplies over two thin ropes. Balancing a load between recruits proved challenging, requiring all to act as one to be successful. Simms and Hill both fell before the squad stopped to assess the situation more thoroughly. Northwood and Smith made a plan to create a pulley system that replaced the use of brute force. Soon the recruits were on the other side.

The final obstacle was the "weaver," and it proved to be the greatest challenge. It was constructed of vertical and horizontally crossed logs positioned to resemble railroad tracks. The "tracks" rose at a forty-five-degree angle to a height of twenty feet before going down the other side. It looked like a huge three dimensional A-frame. The recruits had to go under one log and over the next all the way to the top. The obstacle took a toll on the body, leaving the recruits' shoulders throbbing before they were halfway to the top. Finally, just to make it a little harder, the men were required to move two heavy ammunition cans over the obstacle. Getting the cans to the peak was most difficult and every member of the squad had to help. The second half of the move was easier though, with the cans moving quickly down the opposite side.

As soon as they had completed the confidence-course obstacles, the recruits moved to another reaction course. This was smaller, with only two problems for them to conquer. Now was the time for them to really practice their decision-making skills, because this would likely replicate their feeling after a few days in combat. Marines expect to go ashore and operate against an enemy for at least forty-eight continuous hours. Then, as here on the Crucible, there would be little food or sleep. They would be stressed, and lives would depend on the decisions they might make and on actions taken. All needed to be prepared for this, because all Marines are riflemen first.

There are several dimensions to the saying, "Every Marine is a rifleman." As an expeditionary force in readiness that will probably find itself deployed, the Corps needs to maintain a philosophy that there are no "rear area" Marines. Everyone is close to combat and all need to know how to fight. Experiences from the Chosin Reservoir and Khe Sanh reinforced the effectiveness of this philosophy. Practically speaking this increased the force's combat power, but also reminded each Marine that the responsibility of mission accomplishment was his or her own.

In addition to the marksmanship training with the M16A2 service rifle, recruits participated in Basic Warrior Training (BWT) as an introduction to the combat skills Marines have been noted for since 1775. During the three-day BWT, recruits learn basic field skills from just setting up a tent to field sanitation to movement techniques. Following recruit-training graduation, the new Marines will go home for ten days' leave and then attend Marine Combat Training (MCT) at

Camp Pendleton.[1] MCT is seventeen training days, with fourteen of the days spent continuously in the field. The training schedule covers the infantry skills essential to operate in a combat environment and win on the modern battlefield. Each individual will learn everything from patrolling to offensive and defensive tactics to land navigation to close combat. They will also train with light, medium, and heavy machine guns, as well as with most other infantry weapons found in the Marine Corps' inventory. The purpose of this training is to teach every Marine how to operate as a member of a Marine rifle squad.

The mission of the Marine Corps rifle squad is to locate, close with, and destroy the enemy by fire and maneuver, and repel the enemy attack by fire and close combat. Each squad contains thirteen Marines: a squad leader and three fireteams of four Marines apiece. The squad utilizes a variety of weapons and equipment to accomplish its mission.

With the massive amount of firepower available to the individual Marine, and the potential for his actions to be of strategic significance if captured on live international television, it is important that each Marine develop the ability to make quick and accurate decisions. The Crucible helps lay a foundation for these recruits to build that ability to fight smart. It will be enhanced at follow-on schools and for their entire time in the Corps.

At the first reaction-course station, the squad was delivering a canister of decontamination fluid to a chemical-decontamination team. They came to a hastily constructed minefield, but the remnants of a fence allowed for safe passage. A single bar was awkwardly positioned over the minefield. They had two ropes and a fifty-five-gallon drum representing the decontamination fluid. All they needed to do was to get the fluid to the team on the other side.

1. Parris Island graduates attend MCT at Camp Lejeune, North Carolina. Officers attend the Basic Officer's Course at Quantico, Virginia, after Officer Candidate School. The officer training lasts for six months and is designed to give every officer, regardless of military occupational specialty, the training necessary to serve as a provisional rifle-platoon commander.

Hill stood on the barrel and jumped to the bar, several feet away. He placed himself on top so the others could throw him one of the ropes. Hill tied the rope to the bar, then swung across. The others were now able to swing from one side of the minefield to the other, and began to do so. The second rope was wrapped around the barrel so it could be tied to the swinging rope. They easily accomplished the mission.

On the second obstacle they had two fifty-five-gallon barrels that another unit needed for fuel, but a partially destroyed bridge prevented them from driving across with a vehicle. Parts of the bridge remains were booby trapped and had to be avoided. They had one rope to use.

The recruits formed a human chain, using the rope to tie to some who were in hazardous positions. Then, the squad passed the barrels across, again, easily accomplishing their mission.

It was 1730 by the time the recruits completed the reaction course. After a little less than a mile-and-a-half hike to the bivouac site, the squad took advantage of a break that allowed them to tend to their personal needs. Sleep was not possible and there was no food, so after a quick cleaning of their weapons they began to focus on their feet, where painful blisters had grown. Medical personnel carefully checked each recruit to determine if anyone was not able to continue. Those told that they had to stop were dealt a painful blow, for they would not be able to continue with their squad.

19

Nighttime Resupply Hike

The nighttime ammunition resupply hike required the recruits to step off on a forced march shortly after dark. They hiked one and one-half miles to a site where there were many heavy ammunition cans and crates that they had to carry back to the bivouac site. There was little thought required for their actions, because the event was more of a "gut check" than anything else.

Not everyone had something to carry, so there was some opportunity for rest. That took a toll on the recruits, because it was easy to slip into a selfish shell and avoid the burden of helping the other squad members. To be successful, all of the men would need to overcome such thoughts and unselfishly sacrifice their own comfort for the team. If everyone failed to actively participate and rotate through the group carrying the ammunition, then progress would suffer and the mission would not be accomplished, as well as engendering ill will among the individuals making up the team.

Hill and Simms, the strongest of the recruits, took very few breaks and served as the backbone of the squad. Waters and Smith were weak and needed to be relieved more quickly than the others. Mascuzzio was suffering from painful sores on his feet, and although he tried to participate, the others would not let him. Completing the march in shape to continue the Crucible was challenge enough for him. The others knew they would have to carry his load or risk losing a teammate.

The pain from the more than forty-two hours of continuous operations affected everyone; all had something that was causing pain and discomfort. For some, their feet hurt, while others had sore knees, shoulders, or elbows. Those without an actual injury had nothing to distract them from the discomfort of their heavy field packs or hungry stomachs. All suffered in various ways.

When the night resupply had been completed, the recruits prepared to get some precious sleep, their last bit as recruits, for tomorrow they would for the first time be known by the title "Marine." The recruits of 4th squad were tasked, however, with part of the night's security watch, meaning that each had to stand in the cold Camp Pendleton wind and suffer through an hour of guard duty. The gusts off the Pacific Ocean swirled across the high-water mark toward the canyons of the base. As the wind hummed in off the waves, the spirit and soul of the Corps came with it just as for hundreds of years Marines have come from the sea to fight.

Sergeant Lee collected the squad before they caught some sleep. He reminded them of what tomorrow would bring, and pointed out how proud he was of their accomplishments through the past forty-five hours. Sergeant Lee also told the squad about a recruit from another platoon that had been caught stealing food earlier in the day. The recruit was now packing his gear and being removed from the company, maybe even recruit training. He will be charged with violating the Uniform Code of Military Justice (UCMJ), and the company commander recommended that he be discharged from the Corps immediately. The recruit lacked integrity, and didn't have the honor required to be Marine.

"Tomorrow you claim the title. You'll each be Marines. But with that title will come new responsibilities. Those of you who might view tomorrow as the end have the wrong idea. This has been the easy part. The real challenge will be how you do after you leave recruit training. It's taken three months for all of you to come this far, but that time has been under the direct control of your drill instructors. In the future you will need to continue to do the things that have brought you to this point, but you'll do them without us on your butt making you perform and striving to improve. Every day you'll need to get up and earn the title again, but, unfortunately, you'll come across some who have stopped earning the title. Some of you may come to that point yourself, and statistically not all of you will make it through your four-year enlistment. So you need to think tonight about how far you've come. Think about how much has changed since you got off that bus in your civilian clothes with your long hair. You need to capture this moment in your memory and be prepared to relive this night every time you hit the rack and prepare to get up and re-earn the title 'Marine.'"

By now it was almost midnight and the recruits were forty-six hours into the Crucible. They were completely exhausted, but were also intoxicated with excitement about the next day. There would only be four hours of sleep and 4th squad would get only a maximum of three because of their guard duty. What little sleep they did get would not be enough to reenergize their fatigued bodies. That might prove to be a problem, because they would confront the most demanding challenge tomorrow.

20

Climbing Mount Suribachi

In 1945, the Corps' strength was nearing 475,000, spread across six Marine Divisions. They were preparing for their toughest battle ever—Iwo Jima. It was a nasty little island: five miles long and two-and-a-half miles wide, with black volcanic rock and sand, and reeking of the smell of rotten eggs (Iwo Jima means Sulfur Island). Shaped like a pork chop, the island was covered with scrub vegetation and hills that resembled rock quarries. The few beaches available to support the landing were dominated by Mount Suribachi, a 556-foot extinct volcano.

Iwo Jima was strategically important as an air base for fighters escorting long-range bombers headed for mainland Japan. It would also provide an emergency landing strip for crippled B-29 bombers returning from attacks on Japan. The seizure of Iwo Jima would allow for a more intense air campaign, improve the Navy's capability for sea blockades, and deny the Japanese use of two more airfields.

Initial attacks on Iwo Jima came in the form of carrier raids and began in June 1944. The island would suffer the longest and most intense bombardment of any island in the Pacific during the war, but the 23,000 Japanese troops defending it knew that the island was the gateway to Japan. Hundreds of concrete blockhouses and thousands of smaller pillboxes were constructed. Caves were linked by tunnels, and ammunition and supplies were distributed to remove the need for resupply during battle. The Japanese fortified Iwo Jima to near perfection, planning to make the Marines fight for every rock by dying in place after killing as many Marines as possible. In the end it would become the costliest battle in Marine Corps history with more American casualties than Japanese.

On 19 February 1945, Marines on 450 ships ate a traditional breakfast of steak and eggs and loaded into their landing crafts for the movement to Iwo Jima. Naval guns put the final touches on the three-day preinvasion bombardment, and at 0859 Marines of the 4th and 5th Divisions hit the beaches. The initial wave landed with little resistance, but soon the entire beach was ablaze with deadly machine-gun, mortar, and rifle fire from an invisible enemy. The numerous cliffs along the coast made choices of landing beaches few, and the Japanese knew where to register their fires. Vehicles sank in the soft volcanic sand and became stuck. Several of the tanks hit mines. Men struggled to seek cover, but the fighting holes they dug refilled almost instantly. The beaches were cluttered with men who were dead or wounded and vehicles that were burning or disabled. Still, the Marines moved forward.

Corporal Tony Stein improvised a machine gun from a downed Navy plane and attacked pillbox after pillbox barefooted. He killed twenty enemy soldiers and made eight dangerous trips to the beach for more ammunition. Gunnery Sergeant John Basilone led his Marines forward by climbing a blockhouse to destroy it with demolitions and grenades. He then led a tank through a minefield while under fire before being killed by a mortar round. Sergeant Darrell Cole single-handedly destroyed four pillboxes with grenades and his machine gun, removing a formidable defense before being killed by an enemy grenade.

It was a bloody first day, with 548 dead and 1,775 wounded by nightfall. The beach was a horrid sight, as the wounded piled up and the surf began to rise. No Japanese had surrendered and the Marines were exposed to their artillery and mortar fire throughout the night. Their tiny beachhead was only 3,000 yards by about 1,000 yards, and they were well short of the day's planned objectives.

The fighting continued on the second day with the same furor as the first. Private first class Jacklyn Lucas, barely seventeen years old, fell on two grenades to save several brother Marines. Corporal Stein was still fighting on D-day plus two despite being wounded. Private first class Donald Ruhl attacked eight enemy, killing one with the bayonet before shooting another. He went to help some of the wounded, and was heard to yell a warning before he smothered a grenade with his body at the base of Suribachi. Sergeant Ross Gray cleared a path through a minefield and single-handedly killed more than twenty-five enemy soldiers. He moved forward unarmed to use satchel charges to destroy six pillboxes. Captain Joseph McCarthy crossed open ground under fire to destroy two pillboxes before calling to his company to follow his lead. At one point he jumped an armed Japanese soldier, took his weapon, and shot him.

Kamikazes were attacking the fleet at sea in force, and by D-day plus three Suribachi was surrounded by Marines. The cold rain that had been falling for days made movement difficult and caused weapons not to work properly. Lieutenant Colonel Justice Chambers took a machine gun round in the lung after personally leading his battalion for three straight days. He was one of the nineteen battalion commanders to fall while leading the twenty-four battalions fighting on the island.

On D-day plus four, Cpl. Hershel Williams fought for four intense hours, destroying several pillboxes with his flamethrower. Marine patrols searched the volcano. Some moved to the top of Mount Suribachi with an American flag and instructions to raise it. They had a challenging climb to the rim of the crater, on their hands and knees at times. Someone found a piece of pipe to serve as a flagpole. At 1020 on 23 February six men raised the stars and stripes over the island. The flag now flew six hundred feet above the landing beaches, and the Marines cheered as the Navy ships sounded their bells and whistles.

A larger flag was sent to the top of Suribachi and the second flag raising was captured by photographer Joe Rosenthal. The picture captured five Marines and a Navy corpsman plunging the flag into the volcano's crest. A wave of strength crashed through the weary Marines and the Japanese suffered a psychological defeat. The secretary of the Navy, observing the operation stated, ". . . the raising of that flag on Suribachi means a Marine Corps for the next five hundred years."

Even with Suribachi in Marine hands, fighting would continue for a month. More than 71,000 Marines went ashore, more than 26,000 became casualties. Five of the twelve men involved in the two flag raisings on Suribachi would be killed by the time the battle ended on 26 March. Admiral Chester Nimitz summarized the performance best: "Uncommon valor was a common virtue."

By 0500 the recruits had been awake for an hour and were on a nine-mile hike along a hilly trail in Camp Pendleton. This final hike was conducted as a company, so the twenty-four squads of Company I moved together. The rate of movement was at a slow pace, not surprising because the recruits and drill instructors had very little energy left after fifty-one hours of almost constant activity.

The second break on the hike was just outside the Military Operations in Urban Terrain (MOUT) training center tucked away in a small valley. The drill instructors formed the company in a horseshoe formation so Capt. John F. Dunne, the company commander, could say some final words to the company of recruits.

"This is my last opportunity to say something to you before we finish this and you become Marines. When we get on top of the hill you won't hear from any of us officers. It's only fitting that the drill instructors who trained you have the privilege of calling you *Marine* for the first time. The sergeant major, being the senior drill instructor present, will give you your title, and then your drill instructor will give you your first eagle, globe, and anchor.

"But to get to that point you need to do one more thing, climb that hill." Captain Dunne pointed to the intimidating rise in front of the recruits, more than a mile hike and rising more than 450 feet vertically. Worse yet, the route rolled through the hills, requiring them to climb several peaks instead of just one. He called it a hill; to the recruits it looked like a mountain.

Only an organization like the United States Marine Corps would be willing to put something as intimidating as this large challenge at the end of a fifty-four-hour endurance course. The mere sight of the hill was enough to make most people quit, so it was going to be a painful end to the Crucible. Captain Dunne said, "We used to call it the 'grim reaper' back before we had the Crucible in recruit training, but somewhere along the way someone renamed it Mount Suribachi.

"Those Marines who served on Iwo Jima didn't join for education benefits, job training, or opportunity. They knew that their country was at war, and for one of the few times in our nation's history our home was threatened by aggression from another. Pearl Harbor had been bombed years before, and Japanese ships and submarines were reported off the western coast. Even the buildings at MCRD were all painted with camouflage because of the threat of air attack. These Marines joined knowing that they would fight and maybe die. They would leave from ports like the one down in San Diego and have no idea when, if ever, they would return. For years they would be gone from their friends and family, barely able to communicate.

"They went through recruit training about half the length of yours and didn't have the same opportunities as you. For them, there was no Crucible during their boot-camp experience. They went straight to the beaches of places like Guadalcanal, Tarawa, Saipan, and Iwo Jima. Their Crucible had names like *Meatgrinder, Bloody Nose Ridge, Sugar Loaf Hill,* and *Mount Suribachi.* You need to be grateful for the opportunity you've had during the past fifty-three hours, because the lessons you've learned are the same that other Marines had to learn in combat. You were fortunate enough to learn through sweat and pain. They had to learn through blood and death.

"This climb will probably be the hardest thing you've ever done, but remember that it doesn't compare to what the Marines who have come before us did. This is a small challenge on the Marine scale of endeavors. I'll see all of you on top."

Captain Dunne turned the formation over to the Company first sergeant, who issued an American color and Marine Corps flag to the honorman from each series. The honormen were both guides from a platoon, who had been handpicked by the company staff after close observation during the Crucible as the best in each series. It would be their privilege to carry the flags to the top of "Mount Suribachi."

The company stepped off uphill at 0700. Mascuzzio began to fall back almost immediately, but Hill and Northwood walked behind him and practically carried him. Simms quickly came to help, too, rotating with the weaker Northwood. Nol gave Mascuzzio one of his pack straps to hang onto and pulled forward like a sled dog. The effort of the recruits produced only a little physical effect, but the moral inspiration moved Mascuzzio forward. Every step brought with it shooting pain that told him that he had to be hurt, but he still didn't quit.

Waters was not hurt but he too was showing signs of being a possible hike drop. His thighs burned from fatigue and he had to force himself to continue moving forward. Smith offered words of encouragement, not letting him quit. Nushi also came to help, giving Waters a push up toward the top, returning the favor of the skyscraper.

Puckett was the worst, feeling nauseated and thinking he would vomit at any moment. He kept stopping to catch his breath, which was the worse thing he could do, as this made him lose his momentum. It took the combined efforts of Evans, Lacy, and Martinez to get him moving again.

The squad was now separated by fifty meters, intermingled with other squads from their platoon, but they remained together in spirit. As small groups they continued focusing their efforts on those who were having the most trouble. None would be left to struggle alone. The teamwork demonstrated in the past two days continued.

After ten minutes of continuous climbing, Mascuzzio's group broke the crest of the *first* rise. There was a plateau for fifty feet, a miserable excuse for a moving break from the monstrous mountain trail. Waters shook off his weakness at the crest and focused on catching up with Mascuzzio. He didn't want the others to have to use their precious energy to help him carry his own weight.

Sweat drenched their uniforms and began to soak the straps of their field packs. Their skin stung, as the salt-stained patches of white on their uniforms grew larger. The moisture from their bodies mixed with the dried dirt and mud on the uniforms to create a slimy mess. Although each had drunk gallons of water in the past few days, all were dehydrated so the staff had to watch for heat stroke.

"Pick it up, Puckett," yelled Sergeant Lee as he came running toward the group. He met them just before they reached the top of the first rise. "This flat area is your opportunity to catch up."

After a minute of encouragement to Puckett, Lee pushed forward at a jog to catch up with Waters's group. The recruits were awestruck by his example and tried to get Puckett moving faster. Sergeant Lee passed recruit after recruit from the formation, speeding to a run, swerving in and out, motivating the recruits to stop their "lollygagging and nonhacking and move forward."

The second rise was shorter than the first but was also more painful. Chests heaved and choked for oxygen as the recruits continued on their move to the top. Mascuzzio's group passed a recruit from another squad who had passed out on the side of the trail and was now receiving medical treatment from a Navy corpsman. Waters was just a few feet behind the limping Mascuzzio, so most of the squad was moving almost intact.

They were passing the eighteenth minute of uphill movement when a surprise hit the squad. Simms, who'd shown no sign of weakness during the entire Crucible, stopped and tried to sit down. The others attempted to push him forward, but it was Waters who finally grabbed his pack strap and pulled him on. The group focused on helping their strongest member who'd now reached his exhaustion point. Where he had carried many of them for the past fifty-three hours, they were now responsible to carry him during the last.

There was no hope of Puckett catching up with the rest of the squad, but he would still finish. From time to time he stopped and buckled over into violent dry heaves. He probably would have vomited if there had been anything left in his stomach. It actually would have relived some of his pain. After a few seconds he would stand back up, take a few breaths, and begin moving again. He would never quit.

The formation of recruits stretched longer as the men of Company I moved higher and higher. Most would finish as a group, but many would straggle in. All had hit their "wall" and moved well past it at this point. Helmets bit into heads, creating headaches. Their rifles seemed to weigh more than a hundred pounds each in their exhausted hands. They'd come too far to stop now. As long as they didn't stop they would soon be Marines.

After more than thirty-one minutes of climbing the lead elements came to a halt at the base of the final rise. The group would wait for everyone to catch up, so they could go over the top as a unit. This was a team effort and they would finish as they started—together!

21

Marine Corps Emblem Ceremony

"COMPANY, ATTEN-HUT!" The rows of nasty, sweaty, smelly men came to perfect attention at the first sergeant's command. *"PARADE REST!"*

"Let us pray," said the battalion chaplain. "O Eternal Father, we commend to Thy protection and care the *newest* members of our Marine Corps. Guide and direct them in the defense of our country and in the maintenance of justice among our nations. Protect them in the hour of danger. Grant that wherever they serve they may be loyal to their traditions and that at all times they may put their trust in Thee. Amen."[1]

"GOOD MORNING, MARINES!" said the battalion sergeant major. This was his third tour on drill instructor duty and he had more than twenty-five years of service as a Marine.

"GOOD MORNING, SERGEANT MAJOR!" shouted the company of Marines.

For the first time they were Marines, and it was special for each in a unique way. Simms was finally part of something he thought was special. Nushi could now join the rest of his family in their proud tradition of Marine service. Smith was now part of the organization that fascinated him. Mascuzzio finally fulfilled his lifelong dream.

1. The Marine Corps Prayer was written at the suggestion of General Shepard, the twentieth commandant, by World War I hero Bishop Sherill.

Waters proved that he could be one of the few and proud. Hill was headed for a life off the farm. Northwood now had direction in his life. Nol, regardless of his legal citizenship status, was an American. Lacy finally lived up to a true challenge. Evans would have the ability to attempt to live up to his responsibilities. Puckett was now a Marine like his late father. Martinez was off the streets and headed for a better life as long as he never looked back. And, Sergeant Lee experienced a sense of accomplishment that could never be summarized by words.

"Welcome to the Corps and congratulations on your accomplishment," continued the sergeant major. "Though many others have received the title Marine, most people have not. You are now different, and will forever be held to a higher standard than others. The country puts a great deal of trust in us, their Marines, and we will not let them down. You now carry on your shoulders the burden of our country's future. Failure is not an option, so carry the burden proudly."

Following the sergeant major's remarks, a recording of the national anthem was played as the American color was raised. The first sergeant then put the company at ease and began the Marine Corps Emblem ceremony.

"In 1868, the Marine Corps Emblem was adopted by our seventh commandant, Brig. Gen. Jacob Zeilin. The first emblem consisted of an eagle with wings spread sitting on top of a globe of the western hemisphere with an anchor in the background. The eagle represents the nation, the globe means for worldwide service, and the anchor reflects the Corps' naval heritage and traditions. This is the emblem that Marines wear today and the one which you are now presented because of your completion of recruit training and transformation into United States *Marines.*

"You will soon join the ranks of fellow Marines serving our Corps around the world and will represent everything that is great in our country. Marines, give thought to the challenges that you have endured at boot camp, and those you will continue to face and conquer in the future. Also, think of the many sacrifices made by those who have come before you, and the honorable and faithful service they have given to country and Corps.

"You are now a member of our nation's nine-one-one force in readiness. Marines are the first called, the first to arrive, and the first to fight and win. Wear our Corps' coveted emblem with pride and honor not only on your uniform, but also in your heart. Remember, once a Marine, always a Marine. You will carry the emblem with you forever. Senior drill instructors, take charge, and issue the eagle, globe, and anchor to your Marines."

The drill instructors who led each squad through the Crucible now began at the front of the formation and presented the new Marines their first Marine Corps Emblem.

"Congratulations, Simms," said Sergeant Lee. "You're a darn good Marine; I know you'll do well."

Sergeant Lee handed Simms an eagle, globe, and anchor with his left hand and shook hands with his right.

"Thank you, Sergeant," said Simms.

"Welcome to the Corps, Hill. You did a great job."

"Thank you, Sergeant."

"I'm very proud of you, Nol. You're doing something that many who were born in this country would never even consider. Thank you for your service."

"Semper Fi, Sergeant."

"Congratulations, Nushi. I never told you, but I know one of your brothers. I'm sure you'll be at least as impressive of a Marine as he is."

"Thank you, Sergeant."

"Good job hanging in there, Puckett. You showed a lot of heart, and I know your dad is proud of you."

"Thank you, Sergeant."

"I'm glad we didn't let you quit, Lacy, because you're a good Marine. Keep up the hard work and become even better."

"Yes, Sergeant."

"Smith, I have to say that I really saw something new out of you on the Crucible. You're remarkably bright, congratulations."

"Thank you, Sergeant."

"You really sucked it up, Mascuzzio, but I'm afraid you're going to be on limited duty for a while. Don't let that slow you down; keep driving on."

"Thank you, Sergeant."

"Congratulations, Martinez. Remember who you are now, and don't ever look back."

"Thank you, Sergeant."

"Good job, Evans, I think—" Sergeant Lee's words were interrupted by a commotion to his left. Puckett had collasped. "Well, get him stretched out Marines and check his breathing." He turned back to face Evans, "I think you're going to be a good Marine."

"Thank you, Sergeant."

"Congratulations, Northwood, welcome to the Corps. You have a lot to offer, you really showed that the past three days."

"Thank you, Sergeant."

"We've been through a lot together Devil Dog, congratulations."

Waters exploded into tears and was unable to give an audible response. Sergeant Lee gave him a firm shake with his hand and felt a tingling of his own emotion. This was when the impact of his contribution slammed him right in the face. Standing in front of these men, eyeball to eyeball, and seeing how much this moment meant to them was often more than he could control.

"Get Puckett on his feet," said Sergeant Lee to the Marines assisting him. "He's not going to be flat on his back during the singing of 'The Marines' Hymn.'"

"The Marines' Hymn" is the oldest of the official songs of the armed forces. Though its origin is unknown, legend states that a Marine on duty in Mexico in 1847 wrote the original words. The music comes from a Jacques Offenbach operetta from 1859. Regardless, tradition calls for Marines to stand at attention when they hear "The Marines' Hymn." Exceptions to the rule were rare: From the cots of a medical-aid station full of wounded Marines, from the fighting holes on the front lines of combat, or, in one case, Cpl. David Wilcox sang the Hymn repeatedly so rescuers would find him buried under eight feet of rubble from the destroyed Marine barracks at Beirut on 23 October 1983. Puckett stood and sang with the others:

From the Halls of Montezuma
To the shores of Tripoli,
We fight our country's battles

In the air, on land, and sea.
First to fight for right and freedom,
And to keep our honor clean,
We are proud to claim the title
Of United States Marine.

Our flag's unfurled to every breeze
From dawn to setting sun;
We have fought in every clime and place
Where we could take a gun
In the snow of far-off northern lands
And in sunny tropic scenes,
You will find us always on the job—
The United States Marines.

Here's health to you and to our Corps
Which we are proud to serve;
In many a strife we've fought for life
And never lost our nerve.
If the Army and the Navy
Ever look on Heaven's scenes,
They will find the streets are guarded
By UNITED STATES MARINES!

Epilogue

Eleven weeks earlier many of these new Marines had stood in a grim barracks and cried for their mommies, cellulite hanging over the waistbands of their skivvies, unable to speak without blubbering. But now they stood on top of a hill with tight bellies and strong convictions about what they could accomplish if they stopped making excuses. Some still had tears, but now it came from a combination of the delirium and elation of the moment. They were now part of an elite band of brothers and sisters—they were United States Marines.

Although these new Marines accomplished a lot during recruit training, they were only beginning. The Crucible is only a small part of entry-level training, and they would soon find themselves taking on new and more demanding challenges. Each would need to re-earn the title Marine every day if he were to be successful. The transformation was not complete. It was a four-step process: recruiting, recruit training, cohesion, and sustainment. The Crucible helped the process along, but only good old-fashioned Marine Corps leadership would ensure a bright future for these men in the Corps. There was plenty more potential to tap from each one of them.

All Marines, past and present, can be confident that the Corps is innovative in dealing with America's latest generation, while remaining tough enough to accomplish tomorrow's difficult missions. Current Marine leaders are challenged to continue the transformation by seeing that all new Marines are given the models they need. They enter the ranks of the Corps expecting a lot, thinking all Marines are like their drill instructors. They will practically demand substance from their leaders and instantly respect those who set the example.

Some fail, falling into old habits, not finishing their four years honorably. They are different now, an unmistakable fact, but the past three months does not remove the reality that new Marines are still only eighteen or nineteen years old and still have to deal with many outside influences. In a society where multicolored hair, body piercing, disrespect for authority, and public boasting of unlawful conduct makes someone an icon, it follows that there are challenges outside of the uniform, too. These Marines will find themselves walking a fine line, teetering on an edge between completely different philosophies within the same American society. To be successful they will need to continue the transformation that started at recruit training and not give in to the pressure of society.

Many are confronted with the reality of being a Marine within hours of leaving the depot. They return home on their ten days of postgraduation leave and visit friends. Stories of recruit training are told, experiences from the past three months shared, and then a marijuana joint might suddenly appear. A friend may light it and pass it around. Three months ago it would have gone unnoticed, meant nothing, but now the new Marine notices something new. He feels uneasy and is shocked at how different he now is from his old acquaintances. The joint makes its way around the circle until it gets to our Marine. Someone holds it out for him, maybe a pretty girl who he has always liked or a best friend whom he has known his entire life. There are no drill instructors or squad to help. The Marine is alone and faced with a decision.

The Marine says "no," causing a spirited response from his "friends," but he holds his ground. If recruit training has been successful, the Marine leaves. The Corps' policy on illegal drugs doesn't stop at nonuse; it is *no tolerance.* A new kind of culture shock comes over the Marine as he realizes that his "friends" are disgusted at his actions. *Who are you to judge?*

It is a difficult act for a young man, but somehow the Crucible made it easier:

The results of the first iterations of the Crucible have been impressive, not only in the increased sense of pride and maturity in our new Marines, but in other, more tangible, ways as well. For example, liberty incidents of the Crucible-trained companies going through infantry-training battalions at the schools of infantry have decreased dramatically. Both schools report that companies composed of Marines who have completed the Crucible are performing better than Marines who underwent the syllabus prior to implementation of the Crucible. Recruiters report that these new Marines, when assigned to the Recruiter Assistance Program, are more responsible and more confident. These are preliminary results, but clearly we have hit the mark. We have taken a proven process that produces the finest fighting men and women in the world and actually improved it!

—Gen. Charles C. Krulak, Commandant, USMC

Only time and performance on the battlefield will demonstrate the effectiveness of the Crucible. Since 1775 Marines have done two things for the country: make Marines and win battles. The two go hand in hand, for the Marines made today will win those battles of the future.

Very soon these Marines will be in the Fleet Marine Force (FMF) on the pointing edge of America's defense spear, forward-deployed on naval ships and bases around the world. They will continue to be the most ready when the country is the least. For only 6 percent of the defense budget Marines provide much: 12 percent of the active forces, 23 percent of the active divisions, 14 percent of the total tactical aircraft, and a reliable 911 force for the country.

Private first class Simms will go on to the School of Infantry and earn the new title of 0311 rifleman, or "grunt." He is now the Corps' most valuable asset: the individual Marine. He'll join one of the Corps' infantry battalions and can plan on participating in at least two six-month deployments before the end of his four-year enlistment. In nine months he'll be promoted to lance corporal, and in a few years to corporal. Soon he'll be leading and mentoring new Marines; maybe he'll even be a drill instructor one day.

Sergeant Lee will finish his tour on the drill field and return to the FMF as a staff sergeant. As the platoon sergeant for a rifle platoon, he'll use many of the lessons and skills he learned as a drill instructor to further train his Marines. Also, he'll be a valuable right-hand man for a new second lieutenant serving as the rifle platoon commander.

Lieutenant Harris will be promoted to captain, and will attend the Amphibious Warfare School after his tour at MCRD. He'll assume the duties of a rifle-company commander in the FMF and be responsible for the training and welfare of almost 200 Marines. Leading the best during his time at the depot, the drill instructors, developed him into an even better leader than before. His experience will serve the Corps well as he leads his Marines forward.

Each Marine is poised and ready to do anything the country asks of him or her. They advance into harm's way to protect American lives and interests: traveling through the air in the back of a helicopter, through the surf in an amphibious tractor, or over the mountains on their own feet. No challenge seems too large and no enemy is too strong. Against the most hopeless of situations they remain always faithful. They land in places with strange names and perform difficult, often thankless missions, but they don't fight for thanks. They fight for country and Corps, but, in the end, and more than anything, they will fight and die for each other—for fellow Marines. The faces and names of those Marines graduating today may be different from those of years' past, but the heroic spirit embodied in the word *Marine* is the same. As Marine legend Chesty Puller said: "Old breed? New breed? It doesn't make a damn bit of difference as long as it's the Marine breed!"

Bibliography

Anderson, Jon, R. "Marines Show Metal in African Conflicts," *Marine Corps Edition Navy Times*, June 17, 1996.

Anderson, Jon, R. "Marines Rescue Americans From Albania," *Marine Corps Edition Navy Times*, March 24, 1997.

Aquilina, Robert, V., "Two of the Corps' Earliest Medal of Honor Holders Recalled," *Fortitude*, Spring 1991.

Atkinson, Rick. *Crusade: Untold Story of the Gulf War.* Massachusetts: Houghton Mifflin Company, 1993.

Audsley, Walter, W., Capt., USMC. "Sir, We Have a Fire Back Here!" *Marine Corps Gazette*, October 1996.

Davis, Burke. *Marine! The Life of Chesty Puller.* New York: Little, Brown and Company, Inc., 1962.

Defense Equal Opportunity Management Institute. *Hispanic Heritage Month.* Research Directorate, Patrick Air Force Base, 1996.

Defense Equal Opportunity Management Institute. *A Review of Data on Native Americans.* Directorate of Research, Patrick Air Force Base, 1996.

Defense Equal Opportunity Management Institute. *Women's History Month.* Research Directorate, Patrick Air Force Base, 1997.

Estes, Kenneth, W., Lt. Col. USMC. *The Marine Officer's Guide.* Maryland: United States Naval Institute Press, 1985.

Fleming, Keith. *Corps in Crisis.* South Carolina: South Carolina Press, 1994.

Fuentes, Gidget. "Sink or Swim?" *Marine Corps Edition Navy Times*, December 2, 1996.

Hammel, Eric. *The Root: The Marines In Beirut August 1982 to February 1984.* California: Pacifica Press, 1993.

Heinl, Robert, D., Col., USMC. *Handbook for Marine NCOs.* Maryland: Naval Institute Press, 1988.

Holm, Jeanne, Maj. Gen., USAF. *Women in the Military: An Unfinished Revolution.* California: Presidio Press, 1992.

Hughes, Kelley, S., Sgt., USMC. "Riot Duty in Los Angeles," *Leatherneck,* July 1992.

Jenks, Robert, C., CWO-2, USMC. "Two Marines Die in Oklahoma Blast," *Leatherneck,* June 1995.

Krulak, Charles, C., Gen., USMC. "The Crucible Event: Building Warriors for the 21st Century," *Marine Corps Gazette,* July 1997.

Krulak, Victor, H., Lt. Gen., USMC. *First to Fight.* Annapolis: United States Naval Institute Press, 1984.

Lowery, Timothy, S. *And Brave Men, Too.* New York: Crown Publishers, Inc., 1985.

Millett, Alan, R. *Semper Fidelis: The Story of the United States Marine Corps.* New York: Free Press, 1991.

Moskin, J. R. *The Marine Corps Story.* New York: Little, Brown and Company, Inc., 1992.

Mundy, Carl, E., Gen., USMC. "Paradox of the Corps: '. . . such other duties as the President may direct.'," *Marine Corps Gazette,* April 1993.

Sharp & Dunnigan Publications, Incorporated. *The Congressional Medal of Honor.* Chico, Calif.: Sharp & Dunnigan, 1984.

Simmons, Edwin H., Brig. Gen., USMC. *The United States Marine Corps, 1775–1975.* New York: Viking Press, 1976.

Sledge, Eugene, "Peleliu, Neglected Battle," *Marine Corps Gazette,* January, 1998. (Quantico, Va., Marine Corps Association.)

U.S. Marine Corps. "The United States Marine Corps." Internet, http://www.usmc.com.

U.S. Marine Corps. *Blacks in the Marine Corps.* R. W. Donnelly and H. I. Shaw. History and Museum Division, Headquarters, U.S. Marine Corps, Washington, D.C.

U.S. Marine Corps. *Campaigning.* Headquarters, Marine Corps, Washington, D.C., 1989.

U.S. Marine Corps. *Command and Control.* Headquarters, Marine Corps, Washington, D.C., 1989.

U.S. Marine Corps. *Grenada, 1983.* Lt. Col. Robert H. Spector,

USMC. History and Museum Division, Headquarters, Marine Corps, Washington, D.C., 1987.

U.S. Marine Corps. *A History of Women Marines. 1946–1977.* Col. Mary V. Stremlow, USMCR. History and Museum Division, Headquarters, U.S. Marine Corps, Washington, D.C., 1986.

U.S. Marine Corps. *The Iwo Flag Raising: The Event and People.* Bernard Nalty. Historical Branch, G-3 Division, Headquarters, U.S. Marine Corps, Washington, D.C., 1962.

U.S. Marine Corps. *Leading Marines.* Headquarters, Marine Corps, Washington, D.C., 1989.

U.S. Marine Corps. *U.S. Marines in Lebanon, 1982–1984.* Benis M. Frank. History and Museum Division, Headquarters, U.S. Marine Corps, Washington, D.C., 1986.

U.S. Marine Corps. *U.S. Marines in Vietnam, 1954–1973.* Brig. Gen. Edwin H. Simmons, USMC. History and Museum Division, Headquarters, Marine Corps, Washington, D.C., 1977.

U.S. Marine Corps. *Warfighting.* Headquarters, Marine Corps, Washington, D.C., 1989.